Integrating
Special Education

Integrating Special Education

edited by

Tony Booth and
Patricia Potts

Basil Blackwell

First published 1983
Basil Blackwell Publisher Limited
108 Cowley Road, Oxford OX4 1JF, England

British Library Cataloguing in Publication Data

Integrating special education.
  1.Handicapped children—Education—England
  2.Mainstreaming in education—England
  I.Booth, Tony   II.Potts, Patricia, 19---
  371.9'0942   LC4036.G6

ISBN 0–631–13195–7
ISBN 0–631–13196–5   Pbk

Typesetting by Kerrypress Ltd

Printed in Great Britain by Billing and Sons Ltd, Worcester

Contents

Preface

The idea for this book arose out of a two-day seminar in July 1981 involving the contributors during which we shared our views on the answer to a single question: if we wish to promote integration, how should we set about it? We did not examine, in detail, the different question: should integration proceed? We shared a common commitment to an integration principle: a position that each of us had adopted during our different experiences in working within education. We felt that an examination of *how* integration could be implemented was the best way we could contribute to a debate on *whether* and *to what extent* integration should be pursued. As will become apparent, there was a degree of consensus on how integration might proceed but agreement was far from total. All the chapters have been rewritten specifically for the book and chapters 1 and 13 have been added to set the others in context and fill in the gaps. Only one or two chapters resemble the seminar papers from which they arose. Most of them show how rapidly our views have been extended and revised. But the central commitment to an integrated, comprehensive education system remains as an essential feature of them all.

Some people have suggested that the terms 'integration' and 'special education' are outmoded; that they are themselves products of a segregating system and that a truly integrated education system would have no need for them. But at a time when there is new pressure to recreate a banded education system containing special, vocational, state academic and private sectors, the reality of the segregating forces within education seem more apparent to us than ever. It is to part of the process of reversing this reality that our title refers.

Tony Booth
Patricia Potts

Acknowledgement

We would like to acknowledge the helpfulness and kindness of the library staff at the Cambridge Institute of Education and the Open University.

The Contributors

Tony Booth　Lecturer in Education, Open University

Tony Dessent　Senior Educational Psychologist, Cambridgeshire Education Authority

Jean Garnett　Head of Remedial Service, Coventry Education Authority

Carole Goodwin　Educational Psychologist, Sheffield Education Authority

Neville Hallmark　Head of Heltwate School, Peterborough

Elizabeth Jones　Her Majesty's Inspector, Department of Education and Science; ex-counsellor at Banbury School, Oxfordshire

Neville Jones　Principal Educational Psychologist, Oxfordshire Education Authority

Colin Low　Lecturer in Law and Sociology at Leeds University and active in a variety of organizations of blind and disabled people

Patricia Potts　Lecturer in Education, Open University

John Sayer　Principal of Banbury School, Oxfordshire

Will Swann　Lecturer in Education, Open University

1
Integrating Special Education

TONY BOOTH

Introduction

Integrating children and teachers
In this book we shall define integration as the process of increasing the participation of children and young people in their communities. We see their involvement in the social and educational life of comprehensive nursery, primary and secondary schools as well as further and higher education as an integral part of this process. 'Integration' is most commonly applied to the bringing of handicapped children from segregated special schools into ordinary schools and since they are an excluded group it is appropriate that this should be so. But there are problems associated with such a restricted definition. First, it may imply that the job of involving handicapped children in the educational and social life of schools is finished once they are within the ordinary school building. Secondly, it may be taken to mean that handicapped children have a greater right to participation and an appropriate education in ordinary schools than other children. Integration can be applied then not only to children thought of as handicapped but to all children who have needs and interests to which schools do not respond. The children who are sent to special schools and classes are there, for the most part, because ordinary schools have not adapted their curricula and forms of organization to diverse needs, interests and talents. They pose the same challenge to the education system to become truly comprehensive as the amalgamation of grammar, secondary modern and technical schools.

We have drawn up two continua of integration which may

help to clarify the congruence between the processes of integration and the development of comprehensive education. Table 1 represents the range of provision currently available for children with physical disabilities.

Table 1   A continuum of provision for children with physical disabilities

1	Unsupported member of ordinary class group
2	Child given support in the ordinary class
3	Part-time withdrawal to a resource base
4	Full-time attendance in a special class
5	Part-time attendance at day special school
6	Full-time attendance at day special school
7	Full-time attendance at boarding special school
8	Full-time attendance at hospital and hospital school

At points on this continuum, apart from those at either extreme, the arrangement of a child's education is largely unrelated to the severity of the handicap. There are children with mild physical disabilities in day special schools and there are some with severe disabilities who are supported in the ordinary class group. It is this discrepancy in available provision that forms a major source of information about the extent to which integration of children with disabilities is feasible.

Different groups of children are educated along different continua particularly outside the ordinary school. At one extreme children involved in discipline problems may be taken into care or sent to community homes with education (see Booth 1982a). Once children are within the ordinary school (points 1–4) there are a vast number of possible degrees of participation which are not included in table 1. Their range of contacts with other children may vary in quality and there are a range of ways in which they may be included in ordinary lessons. Table 2 represents an alternative continuum of integration that brings out some of these divisions and represents integration as part of the development of comprehensive community education.

Table 2   An alternative continuum of integration

1   Coming out of special schools
    Gaining entry to ordinary schools
    Becoming full-time members of ordinary schools
    Having positive contact with other children
    Participating jointly in educational activities
    Participating in ordinary lessons
    Participating in academic lessons
    Participating in the core curriculum

2   Reorganizing ordinary schools
    Extending mixed-ability teaching
    Relating the curriculum to the needs and interests of pupils
    Organizing support through team teaching
    Revising the relationship between examinations and the
    curriculum
    Making the core curriculum of the school reflect the
    capabilities and interests of all the pupils

3   Developing community schools
    Using schools as a resource for the whole community

4   Changing patterns of control in ordinary schools
    Sharing control of education between teachers, pupils and
    the community
    Developing patterns of democratic control

5   Delivering education to the community
    Making educational resources freely available to the
    community wherever people need them
    Supplying the means for communities to determine the
    nature of and make provisions for their own educational
    needs

Table 2 is not intended as a set of recommendations but as a
series of issues raised by increasing participation in comprehensive education. It emphasizes the change of power within
education that is a necessary condition of increasing the
participation of pupils, parents and communities in schooling
and a number of chapters return to this theme. Once children
are within ordinary schools the central question for integration

as for comprehensive education is: 'How do we include all pupils within the social and academic core of the school?' Providing an answer to such a question may radically affect our views on the overt (and hidden) core curriculum (see Quicke 1981). It involves a real attempt to define the goals of the school so that they reflect the diverse and common desires, aspirations, interests and backgrounds of all the pupils.

Thinking about the way schools might be organized so that they increase the participation of children involves looking at the extent to which schools can reduce the handicapping effect of a physical or sensory impairment or limited performance or ability on some task. And if schools can reduce failure or alleviate handicap then they can be intimately involved in its creation (see Booth 1982b). Neither failure nor handicap are fixed quantities derived by counting the numbers of children with particular characteristics but are a product of relationships within a social system in which schools are an active component. The numbers of children with special needs within a school will vary with the extent to which the needs of the children are actually being met. Perhaps the best way of thinking of a child *as in need of* special education is in the same way that a child may be *in need of* food. When she has eaten she no longer needs food. Special needs, then, are unmet needs.

We have not attempted to impose or devise any rigid definitions of terms such as 'special educational need' or 'learning difficulty'. The efforts of official documents to control the use of ordinary language are unlikely to be very fruitful. We have felt it appropriate to persist in using the word 'handicap' despite its official disappearance. On the whole we find the term less mystifying than others. A handicap is a burden that impedes someone from reaching a desired goal. Some children *are handicapped* though the source of their burden is often to be found in the social reaction to their bodies rather than in any physical impairment itself. It is true that the use of the word 'handicap' carries a stigma; we believe it is stigma that we should attempt to remove, not words. But there are ways in which the defamation of ordinary language in the 1981 Act may damage the interests of children. Under the Act a child can have 'a learning difficulty if he has a disability which either prevents or hinders him from making use of educational facilities of a kind generally provided in the schools'. If an LEA refuses to make general access to ordinary schools available for gifted children in wheelchairs then they will be said to have 'learning difficulties'. As we shall see, that is not the only instance of an attempt to 'blame the victim' in special education.

As a consequence of treating problems over physical access into buildings as 'learning difficulties' in children, it appears that adaptation to buildings should be viewed as part of the cost of integrating *children*. However most people who are excluded from school buildings because of a lack of access are adults. These include parents or grandparents with disabilities who are unable to participate in their children's education or in community facilities located in the school. Most people with physical disabilities are old people. But perhaps the most significant excluded group are potential educational employees with disabilities: teachers or welfare assistants or child-care assistants or secretaries or support professionals. The effective integration of children with disabilities into education is heavily dependent on a new attitude to the inclusion of adults with disabilities in the workplace of which schools are a part and this may provide the most obvious test of their potential value in the labour market.

Integrating the systems
A number of parents have become concerned about the extension of the term 'special' to cover a sizeable proportion of children within the ordinary school. They are afraid that their children will become stigmatized if the term is applied to them. Such a reaction has implications for attitudes to those children who have been termed 'special' in the past and have been educated, usually, in separate special schools. But there is a real danger that the abolition of a distinction between 'remedial' and 'special' education advocated within the Warnock Report (DES 1978) may lead to more children gaining a specialized, different, education from the majority in ordinary schools. This is Sally Tomlinson's (1982) prediction for the future of special education. The changes we are discussing in this book, however, imply the removal of all forms of selection in education by ability or handicap. It is the abolition of the

distinction between ordinary and both remedial and special education that is implied by our application of the integration principle.

At present special and ordinary education are distinguished by different training routes and pay structures for teachers and by differing management structures as well as differing philosophies and bases of knowledge (see chapters 4, 6 and 12). Several of the chapters in this book explore the possibilities for amalgamating the special and ordinary education systems. But as Neville Jones points out (chapter 4), university special education lecturers and the books they edit are products of these distinctions and we are aware of the contradictions of advocating the abolition of a system while making a contribution within it. It is up to you to judge the extent to which we are damned by our own activity.

The integration debate

Discussions and disputes about integration have been confined, traditionally, to one part of the subject matter of this book; namely whether, which, how many and how children educated in special schools should be brought into ordinary schools. We have not devoted a great deal of this book to agonizing over the debate because we feel that a number of features of the issue can be resolved.

Whether or not children with a wide range of handicaps should be involved in ordinary schools primarily involves a moral choice in the same way that advocacy of comprehensive or grammar schools involves choosing between different kinds of society. Arguments for integration largely rest on the rights of all people to participate in their communities and on the experience of the negative effects that their exclusion has on their lives and those of others. Of course people have to make up their own minds about whether or not they adhere to integration in principle, though advocacy of an integration principle has been official government policy since the war. Once one has made a moral choice about *whether* children with disabilities should be included one can then determine *which* groups these might be, *how many* children might be included and *how* this might be achieved. The answers to these further questions involve both practical, moral and conceptual considerations. Overtly the integration debate has not been about matters of principle but about the practicality, or otherwise, of including handicapped children in ordinary schools. Now as I have argued elsewhere (Booth 1981) a belief in integration in principle involves a commitment to put it into practice. Much of this book is an attempt to answer the question: if we want to integrate, how might we achieve it?

The arguments in favour of segregation in special schools for some children can be divided into two groups: those that genuinely imply the separation of one group of children in a different kind of school from others of a similar age because of their mental or physical characteristics or learning needs; and, secondly, those that support a view that special provision for some children has to be centralized. Clearly the centralization of resources can occur, physically, within either an ordinary school or a special school, although such centralization does mean that some children would not attend their neighbourhood school. A considerable amount of confusion has arisen because of a failure to separate the two strands of the segregation argument. It is a confusion which lies behind arguments or studies that attempt to show that one place of education is intrinsically more efficient than another. Peter Mittler (1979) has suggested that: 'The question of whether mentally handicapped pupils should be taught in special or ordinary schools should be seen as one of reconciling the child's educational and learning needs with the need to maintain contact with ordinary children in the community' (p.101). Yet the mechanism by which the place of children's education can impede their progress is left obscure. The progress of the children in either place might depend on such things as the children's sense of well-being, what they learnt from other children, the proficiency of staff and the involvement of parents.

The provision of special education would not require a separate school building unless the isolation of a group of similarly categorized children were seen as an essential feature of the education they were to receive. The isolation of the children might be advocated for their own protection, for the protection of others, as a punishment or because a definite educational benefit is likely to be derived by such a separated

grouping. It is hard to sustain an argument that placing groups
of children together in 'maladjusted' provision could actually
be for their own benefit. They are often with children who are
most likely to exacerbate their own problems. Such education
is frequently not desired by the children or their parents and
children are usually placed there in order to relieve tensions
within the ordinary schools. Some deaf adults argue that the
perpetuation of the deaf community depends on the continued
existence of boarding education for the deaf. Advocates of
ESN(S) schooling argue that such schools offer protection
from a prejudiced world and that they are the foundation and
insurance for advances in the education of the severely
mentally handicapped children, advances that only started
after 1971 in England and Wales when they became the
responsibility of the education system. (A similar move
occurred in Scotland in 1974, but in Northern Ireland mentally
handicapped children are still the responsibility of social
services departments.) I shall look in greater detail at the
integration of these three groups in the second section.

But most arguments for segregated education are arguments
for centralization of special education. Adherence to a
principle of integration implies that centralization as well as
separation be kept to a minimum and that a continuous effort
be made to decentralize resources. Several chapters in this
book refer to the provision of closed units within schools,
which mirror special schools within an ordinary school
building, and efforts that can be made to establish a flexible
resource base. No LEA has systematically tackled the extent to
which children from special schools *or* units *or* who receive
resource base support can actually be enabled to return to their
neighbourhood schools. The response to such issues may
reflect geography as much as morality. In country areas any
degree of centralization may involve an unacceptable distance
between children and their community. In Norway where the
choice is often between a small local school or boarding
education because of difficulties of winter travel, integration is
seen in terms of support in the local school.

It is hard to make any predictions about the necessary degree
of centralization in advance of the implementation of an
integration principle. While the integration debate has been

conducted almost universally in terms of children brought in from outside the ordinary school, the application of the principle involves an end to the process of *exclusion* of children from ordinary schools. If fewer and fewer children were to be excluded from their neighbourhood schools then a new degree of 'acceptable' centralization would constantly be evolved.

Everyone involved in discussions of integration in education knows about the reservoirs of emotion that are released in some people. For some professional groups integration implies a shift in responsibility and power. Others see the inclusion of a new wave of children in their schools as an intolerable burden. Parents of handicapped children may be afraid of reopening an emotional wound which surrounds the birth of a handicapped child and their agreement that she should be separated from others in school. If they advocate integration they may be told that they are failing to come to terms with their child's handicap. Some people feel a general unease provoked by unexamined feelings of prejudice. I am not going to attempt a full account of why this subject should sometimes cause such turmoil but the fact that it does has to contribute to our understanding of the issue.

Integration in school and community
To the extent that integration *is* about the participation of children with disabilities in ordinary schools, this has to be seen as part of a wider process or struggle for participation in the community. In the United States the rights of people with disabilities to share in community life were specified in section 504 of public law 93–112 which enacted their constitutional right to access to any facility supported by federal funds. When the integration law, PL 94–142, was passed in 1975 it elaborated and extended into education the earlier legislation. Discussions of integration in the United Kingdom have rarely been based on an acceptance of the rights of people with disabilities, and the absence of access to public buildings and transport is a physical reminder of the limited extent to which we are willing to include people with disabilities and the low priority we give to assessing their needs *as defined by themselves*. How much time do professionals devote to the provision of access for their clients?

Who can be included in ordinary schools?

Are there children who cannot be included effectively within ordinary schools because of the difficulties they present to teachers or the disabilities they possess? According to the 1981 Act all children are to be included in ordinary schools unless this is not financially viable, interferes with the instruction of other children or is incompatible with them receiving the education they require. Now, as I have argued, there are obvious conceptual arguments against 'isolation' as a necessary feature of the education of most children who are currently excluded from ordinary schools. But we can also apply a simple practical test to determine whether a particular group of children can be included. If a group can be incorporated effectively into ordinary schools in one area of the country then it makes no sense to argue that they cannot be included in another comparable area. Such an argument would imply that one or other authority was in breach of the law. In the appendix to this book we have included a selected bibliography of accounts of integration schemes in the United Kingdom. Approaches to integration, in other developed nations, are described in T. Booth (1982c), and Organisation for Economic Cooperation and Development (1981). An examination of these examples produces a number of general conclusions. First, children can be educated within ordinary schools irrespective of the severity of their handicap. Secondly, once a scheme is started, it is no more difficult to include children with severe mental or physical handicaps than children with 'mild' handicaps provided they are given the appropriate level of support. Thirdly, integration has to be seen as a continuous process. It is always possible to increase the participation of a group of children in a school as is demonstrated in the scheme for children with sight difficulties described in chapter 3 or that for deaf and partially hearing children described below.

However, a recognition of the continuous nature of the integration process reveals that the feasibility of integration cannot be determined in a simple mechanical fashion. For in adhering to an integration principle or in attempting to implement the 1981 Act the imperfections in a scheme would not be evidence of the implausibility of integration but evidence for how it might be improved.

But an examination of the conceptual and practical evidence does lead to some precise implications. If one adheres to a principle of integration the vast majority of children currently in special schools would be educated in ordinary schools: 56,000 out of a total of 123,000 full-time special school population were in ESN(M) schools in 1981. Now, in fact, many of these children may be excluded from ordinary schools because some teachers have found them difficult to control, but there would seem to be few justifications for maintaining any separated provision for children with what are now called moderate learning difficulties. The difficulties they have in learning are no different in quality, and often degree, from those of many children who remain within the ordinary school system and the obvious solution is to redirect resources to support them in ordinary schools. Now whilst an application of the integration principle would lead to a phasing out of almost all segregated provision, there are three groups that I would like to discuss in greater detail because of the particular issues they raise: children with hearing difficulties, the disaffected and maladjusted, and the severely mentally handicapped.

The integration of the deaf
There are important and specific issues associated with the education of deaf and partially deaf children, and moves towards integration have been seen by some deaf adults as an assault on their communities, identities and language. P. Ladd (1981) has written a striking account of his experience and views of mainstreaming and his opinions are all the more pertinent for the fact that he was regarded as an oral success in his school years:

> My experience of mainstreaming in England . . . leads me to believe that it is . . . the most dangerous move yet against the early development of a deaf person's character, confidence and basic sense of identity. Forceful, clumsy attempts to mainstream not only deny the facts about being deaf but destroy much that deaf

people and their friends have worked so hard to create
and may in the last resort be seen as genocidal. (Ladd
1981, p.405)

Ladd uses 'genocidal' in a literal sense to refer to the practice of
advising parents against having children or to have an abortion
if their offspring are likely to be deaf. His view of integration is
shared by S. F. Turfus who wrote:

It is highly convenient for oralist educators, as it provides
an opportunity to move children from schools where sign
language is once again being used, thus forcing these
schools to close. The deaf community of the United
Kingdom values these deaf schools highly, as they are
centres where pride and culture are built. They have been
in existence for as long as 140 years and are cornerstones
in the structure of the deaf community. (Turfus 1982,
p.10)

Both these authors refer to the virtual disappearance of the
use of sign language from recent education for the deaf in the
United Kingdom and the consequent exclusion of deaf adults
from the teaching profession. The official means of
communication in schools for the deaf has been spoken
English and there have been deliberate efforts to prevent
children signing, a practice which often reasserted itself the
moment the teacher's back was turned. In preventing deaf
children from using their simplest and most natural form of
communication, teachers have sometimes stunted the growth
of their ideas and vocabulary and impaired their ability to read
and write. Some adults have made startling progress when they
have switched to total communication using both signing and
speech and lip-reading. These and other authors detect a new
move towards the introduction of total communication in deaf
education and are fearful that integration will prevent this
trend and that 'the closure of schools for the deaf will
effectively close the doors of the teaching profession for ever'
(Turfus 1982, p.10).
   There is no doubt that the prejudice against sign language
still operates. In reporting on special centres for the hearing

impaired in ordinary schools Hegarty and Pocklington (1982) argue that:

> the central goal of developing pupils' ability to communicate, preferably in an oral way, is no different from that of deaf education in general; the fact of being in an ordinary school made little difference to the educational objectives. Teachers in all three centres would claim to be seeking to provide their pupils with the means to communicate linguistically with hearing people in a predominantly hearing society. (Hegarty & Pocklington 1982, p.158)

Sign language was viewed as a last resort 'for the small minority who have failed to make any noticeable progress in acquiring oral language'. The wish to promote oralism has led, frequently, to a separation of deaf and partially hearing children and sometimes the view that deaf pupils might have a bad effect on their fellow students with slightly better hearing has been made quite explicit:

> There would appear to be general agreement in the world of deaf education that having profoundly deaf pupils alongside the partially hearing makes for difficulties . . . even apart from their failure to achieve some form of oral capacity, staff were concerned that such pupils, though in the minority, were having a disproportionately negative effect on the functioning of the centre. . . . The teacher in charge claimed that there were at least nine children who 'linguistically could be good partials' but not one was attaining anything like his or her true linguistic potential. The presence of profoundly deaf children – even though by that stage provided for in their own fairly self-contained class – was held responsible to a considerable degree. (Hegarty and Pocklington 1982, p.160)

The insensitive attempt to 'blame the victim' evident in this passage is striking, as is the characterization of the hearing impaired as 'notoriously poor' in social skills or that the 'ignorance of the basic principles of socialising . . . leads to their getting into fights more often . . . bringing trouble upon themselves with hasty or ill-judged reactions' (Hegarty and Pocklington 1982, pp.167, 176). But I would argue that the separation of deaf children and adults from the mainstream of education is itself a product of prejudice and permits mistaken views of deaf people to persist, though clearly these are not removed by surface integration. The recognition of the voice of deaf adults is itself part of the integration process, which is helping to dispel myths for example about the value of lip-reading or about the use of hearing aids which may be of greater benefit to their manufacturers than to deaf children:

> Hearing aids are getting better and better, they are technically more beautiful every day. Unfortunately, behind most hearing aids in a school for the deaf is the same old defective ear which does *not* improve year by year. Thus the improvement is marginal and is no benefit whatsoever in acquiring meaningful language through listening in the vast majority of cases of profound deafness. (Holmes 1981, p.400)

I am convinced that deaf children need contact with other sign language users and that deaf adults should not be excluded from the teaching profession though I think they have something to offer all children. But I do not think that such centralization should occur in what for most deaf children in special schools means a boarding education where children may still be sent at a very early age. The 'side by side' arrangement of special education, in which groups of handicapped children with severe and profound handicaps are centralized in selected ordinary schools, is quite common in some areas of the United States. In such schools there may be an active attempt to foster relationships between children with and without disabilities and extend the community of sign users. Keith Pocklington described a visit to one such school in Michigan:

> Deliberate steps are taken to educate able-bodied and hearing pupils about handicap; they try out hearing aids, crutches and wheelchairs; and some ordinary pupils learn

the rudiments of a manual system of communication. Handicapped pupils, for their part, are encouraged to talk openly about what it is to experience, for example, muscular dystrophy or to have seriously diminished hearing. While this may give the impression of a 'freakshow' in fact it is carried out quite naturally and reflects the more open attitude toward handicap that the Americans adopt. Extensive use is also made of the 'buddy system' whereby ordinary pupils chosen for their sensitive manner and sensible behaviour, are teamed with particular handicapped children whom it is felt experience difficulty in developing relationships. (Pocklington 1982, p.389)

At another school in Madison, Wisconsin, groups of hearing-impaired and non-hearing-impaired children are often combined for team teaching:

A regular education teacher with 20 first and second graders teams on a daily basis with a teacher of the hearing impaired with five hearing impaired children . . . the teacher of hearing impaired children may work with a group of five children, three of whom may be hearing impaired . . . at the same time, on the other side of the room the regular education teacher may work with a reading group of seven children; six non-hearing impaired and one hearing impaired . . . Since the hearing impaired program at Glendale School focusses on total communication (oral language in combination with signing) the grade level teacher as well as the non-handicapped students learn signing and finger spelling. (Gruenewald and Schroeder 1979, pp.28–9)

The junior school containing one of the classes described by Hegarty and Pocklington (1982) was taken over by a new headteacher who has transformed the method of working and the attitudes of both staff and pupils. She did not regard the situation she found as an integration failure but as a problem to be overcome in the same way as she had altered the 'resource area' for visually impaired children described in chapter 3 (and banned the word 'unit' from the school!). Children were attached to ordinary registration groups and team teaching and minimum withdrawal introduced.

P. Ladd (1981) has himself argued that integration can be made to 'work well for everyone's benefit' if the following conditions are met:

1 There should be a tutor/sign language interpreter to aid communication and understanding and to facilitate friendships with hearing children and teach them the language.
2 Clubs where they can meet other deaf children and adults as well as hearing children should be set up for children from age one.
3 Deaf adults should be involved in running integration schemes.
4 Deaf adults should be involved with children's families from as early an age as possible.
5 Deaf teachers should be appointed to the schools.
6 Deaf children should be exposed in a carefully structured way to signing and English from birth.
7 Counselling and social work facilities should be readily available as should be residential courses run by deaf and hearing people.

Of all the items in this list perhaps the most important is the involvement of deaf adults in decision-making and teaching which could ensure that the other necessary conditions were also developed.

The disaffected and maladjusted

The second group that deserve special consideration are children who are placed in schools for the 'maladjusted' or attend disruptive units. The majority of this group are placed after relationships with a teacher or group of teachers have broken down within the ordinary school. They represent the one area of special education that is still undergoing major expansion in England and Wales. Some new special schools for the maladjusted are being opened but the majority of new provision has been in a large variety of special classes, both on the site of and separate from ordinary schools, popularly known as 'sin bins'. Many of the children have been suspended from schools or are regular truants. They may have been involved with the juvenile courts and they may have attended or move on to community homes with education. Although, in fact, they arrive in special provision for many reasons they comprise pupils which ordinary schools are least willing to reintegrate and are often regarded as the hard core of segregated pupils.

Despite their numerical importance the recent NFER study actually omitted these pupils from their study of integration. I would argue that that was a major mistake for three reasons. First, because the factors within schools which give rise to disaffection and produce high rates of suspension and referral to maladjusted provision may be the very same problems which lead schools to exclude children with learning difficulties or physical, mental and sensory handicaps. [All these children challenge the capacity of schools to adapt their curricula and form of organization to diverse needs and interest] Secondly, because the adaptations which schools can make in order to reduce disaffection or include children from maladjusted provision may be those which will facilitate the real participation of children with other difficulties. All other groups can be attached to the ordinary school after the limpet model described by Neville Jones in chapter 4. In order to absorb disaffection, schools can change in one of two ways: they can become more authoritarian and aim to reduce deviance or rebellion by more effective policing and punishment, or [they can become more flexible and adapt to a wider range of needs and interests.] Which solution one chooses, however, depends on one's own view of what a good school should be like. But if integration is linked to participation in school life it is clear that it implies a greater involvement of pupils in determining the content and goals of their schooling; a looser though not less orderly style of education.

The third reason for including 'disaffected' children is closely related to the second. Children who are brought into ordinary schools from special schools for children with moderate learning difficulties, for example, may simply be redefined as disruptive or become disruptive if the appropriate adaptations are not made in the schools. Integration can only be said to be occurring in an area if the overall numbers of children excluded from schools are being reduced.

There can be little doubt that a concerted policy could begin to reduce the burgeoning exclusion of children to disruptive units or maladjusted provision. The excluded children do not form a homogeneous group. Children have been suspended from school for requesting to wear long hair or protesting about sexist literature as well as for fighting or disrupting lessons (Grunsell 1980). In one study teachers placed 'deliberate rejecting of school standards in dress' as the most frequent 'seriously disruptive' behaviour (Mills 1976). The reasons for referral to disruptive unit and maladjusted school show a similar variation and the numbers involved vary from school to school and county to county not just in relation to inner-city problems, poverty or unemployment (see Galloway and Goodwin 1979). Now I am not suggesting that problems of discipline, disruption and disaffection can be made to disappear but that the only appropriate way to tackle them is by an LEA-wide policy which starts from an assumption that such problems cannot be solved by removing an ever-increasing number of pupils from the schools. The head in a large community comprehensive in an impoverished area of Glasgow argued against the setting up of units for disruptive pupils on the grounds that 'teachers are only human. They'll always be able to find ten more pupils they would be happier without.' If a freeze were put on the setting up of new segregated provision and all the time and energy currently expended on referring children, assessing them and moving them out of ordinary schools were spent instead on reducing exclusion rates, then we could gradually redirect resources for the majority of these pupils back into their schools. In the Glasgow school I mentioned they have introduced a school panel where parents and children who are experiencing difficulties with their education attempt to work out with their teachers and others how schooling can be made to satisfy their needs. (See TV 7, 'Pack up your troubles', Open University course E241, 'Special Needs in Education'.) Rob Grunsell has been working on materials for school-based in-service education which could form part of an LEA policy on reducing suspension, disaffection and referral to maladjusted provision and disruptive units.

The severely and profoundly handicapped

In a television programme made for the Open University (TVI 'Just one of those things', E241, 'Special Needs in Education') the father of a profoundly mentally and physically handicapped girl explained the effect on him, his daughter and the other children of her being in a unit for mentally handicapped children attached to an ordinary school.

> It's done wonders for her . . . we went to the baths and there was a couple of young children there, now I didn't know them but they knew Susie because they were from her school and they were talking to her as if she were a normal child. It's very interesting really . . . In today's society where they are integrating these children they obviously will become more used to them and accept them better.

However, Susie's school in south Derbyshire is the only ordinary school I have come across which includes such profoundly handicapped children with no speech or mobility. At first thought it may really seem as if there is little point in integrating such children, as if their low level of social awareness might bring few benefits. Yet, as this father's comment illustrates, in assessing whether such a move has advantages we may have to look at effects apart from those on the child herself; at the reactions of parents who are integrated into the ordinary schools and may have all their children in the same school if they are close to a centralized resource; at the gradual erosion of fears and prejudices within ordinary school children and the community of whom Susie has become a visible part and whose responsibility she will continue to be.

South Derbyshire is one of only two areas in England where severely mentally handicapped children can attend ordinary schools for the duration of their schooling. (From September 1983 this will also become possible in South Oxfordshire.) The integration of mentally handicapped children is a rare occurrence even at the primary level. But this does not mean that where schemes have been established they face any greater problems than those for other groups of children. Published accounts arc available of the schools in south Derbyshire and in Bromley where all the mentally handicapped 3 – 8-year-olds are in ordinary schools (see for example Hegarty and Pocklington 1982; Booth and Statham 1982). Bishopswood ESN(S) School in Oxfordshire has transferred two classes together with their teachers and teaching assistants into a nearby primary school. A group of parents managed to establish a unit for children from ESN(S) schools in a private school when their LEA resisted their campaign to have them in state schools (Booth and Statham 1982).

But the fact remains that there are only a handful of attempts to integrate mentally handicapped children in the United Kingdom and that even where they are integrated for some part of their schooling there are few moves to extend this throughout the school age range (see chapter 3). When Cambridgeshire devised a plan for the future of special education in the county they specifically excluded the mentally handicapped from their discussion of candidates for integration. Why should there be such a resistance to including the mentally handicapped? Mary Warnock has suggested that 'People do not take on board the severely handicapped. It is grotesque to think they could all be educated in ordinary schools.' Yet if some schools do include them why would it be 'grotesque' to expect others to do so?

One clue to the reaction of LEAs to mentally handicapped children in general comes from the prevalent attitude towards children with Down's syndrome. Such children exhibit a wide range of abilities and many of them would not be defined as severely mentally handicapped. Yet in several parts of the country they have been confined to ESN(S) schools because they 'looked mentally handicapped' and some teachers have been afraid that their school would gain a reputation for being 'a mentally handicapped school'. Prejudice certainly does surface when ordinary schools include the mentally handicapped. The 'unit' at Pingle School in Derbyshire was referred to by some pupils as the 'mong wing'. One parent voiced her initial fears that her 'normal' severely mentally handicapped child should attend the same school as 'a lot of mongols'. Whilst prejudice may prevent the establishment of schemes for these children, once they are set up the prejudice reduces considerably. And as demonstrated by the headteacher of the deaf unit, mentioned in the previous section, the more the children are made a central part of the school the greater the likelihood of their acceptance by other children.

ESN(S) schools are sometimes viewed as a sanctuary from a harshly prejudiced world. But it would be a mistake to believe that all ESN(S) schools are havens of acceptance. It is very common for ESN(S) schools to be subdivided into the severely and profoundly handicapped with very little mixing between the two groups. J. Corbett (1982) has made a study of one ESN(S) school in which there was a rigid separation between the profoundly handicapped or 'special-care' children and the rest of the school. The school was established in 1971 with two special-care classes which contained a mixture of very active and immobile children. In 1972 these groups were divided into separate classes, one for the immobile and semi-mobile children and the other for 'problem' and very active children. One teacher reported on her experience of special-care class I in 1972:

> Special care I contained the most difficult children. I had between 12 – 14 children, at one point I had 16 and we were always locked in. If a teacher found a child to be a disturbance in the class distracting other children, they were shunted into special care. I had one staff only to help. When I went there the door was locked and there was no programme for us to go anywhere or do anything, but remain locked from nine to four in that room. I had one able girl who I used to take out of the room with me but staff used to be shocked when they saw her and said 'what are you doing here?' and they were the ones who had weeded out their children. I endured that for almost two years with no music, no physio – no resources. We only had one visiting physiotherapist who said that many physically handicapped children were 'too far gone' for treatment. (Corbett 1982)

In 1975 when two new classrooms were added to the school

the less active group were further subdivided into an immobile and a semi-mobile group. Then in 1977 a new special-care group was formed from those children who were 'presenting behaviour problems' in the rest of the school, making a total of four special-care groups. Working with these children was seen as undesirable by some staff within the school and any suggestion that they should be integrated with the others met with hostility. One problem concerned the discrepancy between the extra allowance (a scale 2 post) given to teachers to work in special care and the absence of an addition for welfare assistants who resented the lack of incentive to do what they felt was 'harder work'. They agreed to rotate the special-care work, moving back at regular intervals when they had 'served their time'. The least mobile, most profoundly handicapped group was also least desired by the teaching staff who rarely stayed with them for more than a year. After working in the special-care department for a number of years staff felt that they were labelled as special-care teachers, subspecialists who could not tackle a wider range of duties with other mentally handicapped children. The situation persisted unchanged until 1981 when the headteacher was prompted to reconsider the organization of her school by the arrival of a new pupil:

> An adolescent girl arrived from another borough, and her notes had not yet been forwarded. The headteacher placed the girl in the group which was appropriate for her age and although she proved to be sometimes awkward and ill-tempered, the class teacher was able to contain her. After a short period of 'settling in' she started to develop very rapidly and made pleasing progress showing an interest in many tasks. It was only when her notes arrived some months later, that the headteacher discovered that this girl had been placed in the 'special care' unit of her previous school where she had been regarded as a 'behaviour problem'. (Corbett 1982)

The headteacher became concerned about the self-fulfilling expectations which might be set up within the special-care department and put forward a proposal to 'integrate' these children into the main body of the school. Most teachers were resistant to the change both within the special-care department and in the rest of the school. One special-care teacher commented: 'I think a tremendous amount of thought has to be put into *any* integration – considering benefits/disadvantages to *everyone*.' A second teacher wrote that 'as my children are on behaviour programmes, which need complete consistency, I would not agree with them being put in other classrooms.' The reactions of other teachers ranged from 'totally impractical', 'I disagree with the whole idea', to mildly favourable.

The headteacher revised her plans in the face of this opposition; she placed a few more able children back into the 'mainstream' of the school, created a new language class to 'present a challenge' for one 'special-care' teacher and created a further subgroup within the remaining special-care children to form 'a smaller, very low-functioning group.' Jenny Corbett came to three conclusions on the basis of her study:

1 The original structure of groups, once established, sets a pattern within the minds of the teaching body, which is very hard to reset or revise in any form.
2 Grouping children into a set which contains other children presenting the same or similar problems is not always [or ever?] to their advantage.
3 Teachers who are specialists in teaching severely subnormal children may still display prejudice and ignorance about the needs and characteristics of cerebral palsied, severely subnormal children.

One of the reasons why a selection or segregation philosophy may emerge as an organizing principle within the ESN(S) school is that they exist as one extreme of the continuum of schooling by ability created by the application of this philosophy. And if prejudice exists against children who are visibly different in appearance and are labelled mentally handicapped is it likely to be exacerbated or reduced by their continued separation in schools of their own?

Integration, selection and the comprehensive philosophy

In this book we have defined integration to mean the same as the development of comprehensive education, yet it has not been customary to make such a link in theory or practice. The January 1983 issue of *Forum*, a magazine devoted to the advocacy of comprehensive schooling, does contain a number of articles devoted to this theme. But Circular 10/65 which expressed the intention of the Labour government to establish comprehensive schools containing 'the whole ability range' was issued during a period of unprecedented exclusion of children from ordinary schools because of their 'disability'. In 1955 special schools contained 0.81 per cent of the school population in England and Wales. In 1965 this had risen to 0.96 per cent and in 1975 it was 1.37 per cent. The growth of special classes and, at the end of the seventies, disruptive units contributed to the emergence of a special education empire within the so-called comprehensive system.

Prior to the introduction of comprehensive schooling the British system represented an extreme of selection. At the European Association for Special Education Conference in Finland in 1980 a Polish delegate was dismissive of the Russian category system of dividing children into three groups by mental ability, claiming that the Polish system enabled children to be distinguished into *seven* distinct tracks. In the United Kingdom, however, a banded grammar school in the area of a banded secondary school with ESN(M) and ESN(S) schools nearby may easily exceed the Polish system in its number of divisions.

Norway has had a comprehensive school system with mixed-ability groupings for the compulsory school years since 1920. In the United Kingdom, selection is recent, still an issue which divides people along party political lines, and the changes to a comprehensive system have been relatively shallow. The ethos of the grammar school with its centrality of public examinations still pervades most comprehensives (see chapters 5 and 9) and few are genuinely unstreamed.

The same selection philosophy which underpinned the separation of grammar and secondary modern schools is at the root of the existence of special schools. The grammar schools embodied a desire that the achievement of some children should be encouraged by the 'carrot' of high-status buildings to which high-status staff would be attracted. The existence of low-status education for the class-related categories of moderate educational subnormality and maladjustment which form the bulk of segregated provision is seen by some as the twin pole or 'stick' in such a scheme (see Tomlinson 1981).

Selection and segregation are also justified by the administratively neat view that teaching and learning are best conducted with groups of pupils of similar abilities and interests and that the education of such groups might be most conveniently organized with separate groups of specialist staff working together in distinct buildings. Such a view might have some surface plausibility if the subdivisions were sufficiently numerous to create homogeneity, but as the case study of the ESN(S) school described earlier demonstrates a single special school contains such a varied group of children that a single teaching approach is unlikely to be appropriate for them all. But such a view encounters other difficulties. Even if a group could be identified who required a single teaching style or method it would not follow that this should be provided in a separate building. The value that is placed on separation must therefore be derived from another source.

Despite its limitations the idea of schools containing homogeneous groups of children receiving a common educational diet continues to influence thinking about special education. The 1959 regulations, in force until the implementation date for the 1981 Education Act on 1 April 1983, define as handicapped those children who are unable to cope with the 'normal curriculum' in the schools. The 1981 Education Act makes a similar assumption in defining children as having special educational needs when they require a form of education different from that 'made generally available for children'. But if we expect schools to cater routinely for children with diverse needs and interests then our whole approach to the notion of special needs should change. Special needs are those to which schools do not currently respond. The numbers of children with special needs vary from school to school, not only because of the characteristics of pupils but because of the organization and curriculum of the school.

A comprehensive philosophy
Integration and the development of comprehensive education

require a fresh starting point for schools rather than the uneasy amalgamation of separate systems. They both involve a client-centred approach to education which starts with the question: 'Whose school is it?' A comprehensive school should be open to all the children (and adults) in a community and the extent of the school's responsibility towards the education of children should be unaffected by their capabilities, background, interests or handicap. The comprehensive ideal involves the attempt to meet the personal and common interests of children together within the same school. Integration involves looking at the way schools should be organized if they are to avoid the exclusion of children, as well as at ways to bring in children who are currently excluded.

In changing the starting point for integration many of the central issues in the discussion become transformed. For example, in a comprehensive system the question about how integration should be funded is changed from 'is it financially viable to include this or that group of children?' to 'what is a just division of a school's resources?' In Italy the law specifies that the education of handicapped children should take place in the ordinary classroom and class sizes are reduced and support teachers made available to classrooms which include handicapped students (Booth 1982c). Some Italian teachers have argued that the assignment of special funds to children on the basis of their handicap leads to unnecessary categorization. They have suggested that funds should be distributed solely according to the general needs of the community, with impoverished areas and inner cities getting a larger share. If teachers, and in particular headteachers, in ordinary schools feel an equal responsibility towards all children, then perhaps they can be relied upon to distribute resources according to need. But the variation in the way in which cuts are administered in the United Kingdom, with some schools cutting their remedial support, suggests that British schools are not yet ready for such a system. It may be necessary to employ a funding formula like that in Norway where 10 per cent of the school budget is for adapting the school for children's special needs (though not for grouping by ability) and additional resources can be reclaimed by the school for supporting the education of children with more severe handicaps. Of course much of the teaching and other resources made available for this later group could come from existing segregated provision. But it is a major defect of the 1981 Education Act that it did not attempt to preserve special funds for the wider support of children in the ordinary school.

The limits to progress

Integration is an unending process. There will always be ways in which the participation of handicapped or non-handicapped children in the social and educational life of their schools can be increased. Integration and the reform of comprehensive education involve a succession of stages along the route to full community participation and control in education. The extent to which such a sharing of power will be achieved is transparently a political matter.

Arguments in favour of integration commonly meet with the response that ordinary schools have to put their own house in order before they should include others. In calling for an initial perfection of the ordinary school system a segregated special educational system can be retained indefinitely. But it is only by adapting to the breadth of needs within a community that schools can begin to become comprehensive.

2

Integrating the Visually Handicapped

COLIN LOW

This chapter considers the problems associated with integrating children with a particular handicap, visual handicap. This is worth doing for several reasons: first, it provides a microcosm of many of the opportunities and difficulties associated with the integration of handicapped children generally. In this connection, given the amount of systematic and well-directed pressure that has been brought to bear over a considerable period of time in support of greater integration for the visually handicapped (so far with only very limited success), it vividly illustrates the kind of resistance integrationists often have to face. But second, by highlighting those aspects that are peculiar to a particular handicap group – what might be termed the 'handicap specific' as opposed to the 'common core' elements of the problem – it focuses attention on the need for a strategy which is sensitive to the needs of particular subgroups within the overall category of the handicapped as a whole. Finally, it is particularly worth looking at the visually handicapped at the present time since, in May 1982, the Department of Education and Science called on local authorities, in regional conferences, to carry out, as the first of a series of reviews of provision for different groups of handicapped children, a review of their provision for the visually handicapped to culminate in the promulgation of a national plan by the summer of 1983. This is something for which the Vernon Report (DES 1972) had called a decade earlier. Regional conferences were reactivated for the purpose in 1975, but nothing much seems to have happened as a result. It is to be hoped that the stimulus of declining numbers may possibly have injected the necessary fluidity into the situation to make a restatement of the integrationist position timely and a reorientation of provision possible.

The shape of the problem

According to DES official statistics, there were in January 1981, 975 blind and 2,098 partially sighted children attending special schools, hospital schools, independent schools or special classes at maintained schools, receiving education otherwise than at school or awaiting admission to special school. These figures represent prevalence rates of 1.12 and 2.41 per 10,000 school population respectively. These 'officially identified' visually handicapped children are catered for principally in 32 inevitably small special schools – half run by local education authorities, and half (chiefly those for the blind) by voluntary bodies; 12, all boarding, cater for the blind alone; 16, of which 3 are boarding, for the partially sighted; and 4, all boarding, for blind and partially sighted children together.

Thus special educational provision for the visually handicapped overwhelmingly means separate or segregated provision. Moreover, at least so far as the blind are concerned, separate provision very largely means boarding provision as well. The figure of 80 per cent for pupils boarding at schools for the blind appears low only in comparison with the staggeringly high figure of 97 per cent given by the Vernon Report a decade ago (the comparable figures for the partially sighted are 1971, 42 per cent; 1981, 35 per cent). Tony Booth (1981), arguing from the dropping proportions of the total school population in special schools for the visually handicapped since 1950, has suggested that visually handicapped children appear to be less likely to attend a special school now than in the past. But he himself acknowledges the possibility that this might be due to a fall in the proportion of children with sight difficulties as much as to any change of policy with regard to school placement. This would appear to be what has happened over the last ten years, at the beginning of which time the Vernon Report gave prevalence rates of 1.37 (blind) and 2.66 (partially sighted). Certainly the proportions of 'officially identified' visually handicapped children placed in special schools – 90 per cent for the blind and 85 per cent for the partially sighted – have hardly altered at all since the publication of the Vernon Report a decade ago, and this is surely the relevant statistic to take.

The Warnock Committee (DES 1978) stated that there has been a steady increase over time in the number of handicapped children placed in designated special classes and units in ordinary schools, rising from 11,027 in 1973 to 21,245 in 1977, i.e. from 6.8 per cent to 12 per cent of all children ascertained as requiring separate special provision. The children placed in these classes and units, the committee makes clear, have been mainly those with moderate rather than severe disabilities, but all categories of handicap are represented. So far as the visually handicapped are concerned, the partially sighted have felt the benefit of this trend to some extent, their numbers attending special classes in ordinary schools having risen from 81 in 1973, the first year when such statistics were given, to 205 in 1981. But the blind have hardly been touched by this development at all: no blind children were in special classes in ordinary schools when such information first became available in 1973, and by 1981 there were still only seven.

Warnock also states that placements of children with disabilities in ordinary classes are becoming more frequent, though statistics of these are not available. For some time now, it has been recognized that there is almost certainly a considerable number of children with a visual handicap of some sort in ordinary schools, in addition to those recorded in the statistics as receiving special education; increasing numbers have also been coming to light in hospitals for the mentally subnormal and similar institutions. Only lately, however, have we begun to gain some idea of the size of these groups, at least so far as the educationally blind are concerned. In 1982 Colborne Brown and Tobin were able to identify at least 1,093 such children who were being educated in a variety of units and schools throughout the country outside what might be termed the 'official' blind education system. This finding that there are as many blind children being educated outside the 'blind education system' as in it accords with the picture derived from local authority social services statistics by Jamieson, Parlett and Pocklington (1977). But it would be a mistake to regard many of these placements as representing integration in the sense of full functional integration into the ordinary life and classes of ordinary schools. From this point of view, Colborne Brown and Tobin's description of their study as one of the 'integration of the educationally blind' is really rather misleading, and their liberal use of inverted commas round the word 'integration' shows some awareness of this. Their more neutral formulation 'not attending special schools for the visually handicapped', which they use elsewhere, would perhaps be nearer the mark. In fact only 144 or 14.4 per cent of their discoveries were in mainstream schools or some sort of unit attached thereto. Almost all of the 114 children placed in a mianstream school directly were one-off placements. Some were sixth-formers having moved from schools for the visually handicapped. A substantial number were at infant school, so might not necessarily remain in integrated provision; and the authors surmise that it is probable that some were placed in mainstream schools for other than strictly educational reasons. None of this bespeaks a particularly vigorous growth of integration schemes throughout the land. The great majority of the children identified by Colborne Brown and Tobin (nearly 700 or 69 per cent) were in schools or units for the ESN(S), ESN(M/S) or physically handicapped, or in special care, hospital or hospital school – some in residential placement, but most on a daily basis; and closer analysis of a subsample of 411 cases showed that almost half (47 per cent) had a mental (as well as) a visual handicap, and three-quarters could accurately be described as multiply handicapped.

What kind of a picture, then, is presented by this diversity of circumstances in which visually handicapped children are being educated? On the one hand, we would seem to have an official, comparatively self-contained, 'blind education system', in which about 3,000 visually handicapped children are being educated, very largely in special, often residential, schools specifically for the visually handicapped. On the other hand, there is also a significant number of children with a visual handicap being educated in a variety of settings outside these schools – settings which, by virtue of being outside the officially sponsored blind education system, all too easily give rise to the misconception that the children being educated in them are in fact being integrated into the community. So far as the partially sighted are concerned the contention of integration is probably correct. Colborne Brown and Tobin did not study this group, but Jamieson, Parlett and Pocklington, in their 1972 study, cited local authority social services figures showing that 29.8 per cent of registered partially sighted children aged 5–15 were in ordinary schools. The only questions, then, that arise concern the adequacy of the support they receive and the means of moving more of them from the comparative isolation of the closed official system towards the more open system of provision in the community. But so far as the educationally blind are concerned, there is real reason to question whether the system has not become skewed so as to make for a serious mismatch between provision and need – those who could safely take their place in the ordinary school, were the requisite systems of support to exist, being educated away from the community in the official blindness system, and those who need the services that system has to offer being cut off from it with inadequate support, at least so far as their visual handicap is concerned.

In the rest of this chapter, bearing in mind that it is the education of the blind as opposed to the partially sighted that is usually thought to give rise to problems of such an intractable nature that the only thing to do with them is to sweep them under the carpet, I shall concentrate largely on the problems of the self-contained blindness system, on the rigidity in the system which gives it so much staying power despite those problems, and in particular on what is needed to make the official 'blind education system' more open-ended, capable of releasing people into the community at one end, while at the other end it draws in those who can best benefit from the particular resources that it has to offer.

Further dimensions of the problem

I do not intend to argue the full case for integration here. This has been done many times before, and no one not already convinced is likely to be converted by mere repetition. This chapter is essentially concerned with the question 'how?' not 'whether?'. But it may just be worth observing that the general case for integration has two aspects. The first, insufficiently stressed, is expressive or symbolic in character. Unnecessary segregation from the community represents a derogation from full humanity and citizenship. Secondly, integration also has an instrumental function. Separate socialization breeds attitudes of prejudice, intolerance and self-denigration; and integration, particularly at the formative stage of development, can do much to sweep away the barriers of ignorance and misunderstanding that keep the handicapped and unhandicapped apart, and ultimately lead to discrimination, dependency and an inability to cope.

These considerations apply in full measure to the visually handicapped. Going to an ordinary school helps a visually handicapped child to grow up and learn to cope with life as a member of a sighted and not a self-enclosed 'blind' world in the most practical way possible – by living in it. It also fosters in the sighted an appreciation of visual handicap as a wholly normal incident of human diversity instead of something alien, to be at best uneasy about or at worst to reject. But integration holds several other quite specific advantages – indeed imperatives – so far as the visually handicapped are concerned. The chronically small numbers concerned inevitably mean that the self-contained 'blind education system' has a number of inherent limitations: it is forced to operate at a regional or even a national level. We have already seen that this entails an extremely high proportion of children having to board away from home for the whole of their schooling. Even so, many of the schools involved, especially those for the partially sighted, still have to cover the entire age range to attain viability; and in order to mobilize the resources necessary for more advanced work, a rigorous system of 11+ selection is more or less obligatory. The very fact of being a self-contained system also has serious drawbacks: as the National Federation of the Blind and Association of Blind and Partially Sighted Teachers and Students (1973) have shown, the special school, particularly the residential special school, has major disadvantages as a setting for the co-education of the sexes, for educating blind and partially sighted children together and for educating visually handicapped children in conjunction with children suffering from other kinds of handicap.

Much of this is often thought to be unavoidable on account of the extremely small numbers involved – there simply are not enough children to make viable primary, let alone comprehensive, schools on anything remotely approaching a neighbourhood basis. And the problems will become acute as numbers decline still further. The DES (1982) has projected numbers for the 'official' system of no more than 700 (blind) and 1,600 (partially sighted) by the end of the decade. But as can readily be seen, this is only a problem as long as it is decided to retain a self-contained system of schools for the visually handicapped alone, more or less completely separated from the rest of the educational system. If blind and partially sighted children were educated in ordinary local authority schools, it becomes immediately obvious that it would be possible for them to receive a normal primary and comprehensive secondary education much closer to home. Indeed the National Federation of the Blind and the Association of Blind and Partially Sighted Teachers and Students (1973) have estimated that if resource centres for the visually handicapped were established in as few as 40 primary and 40 related secondary schools strategically located throughout the country, 82 per cent of the visually handicapped school population could live well within daily travelling distance of their homes – a figure that rises to 95 per cent if 52 centres of each type could be established. It is obvious, too, that by bringing visually handicapped education much more into the educational mainstream, visually handicapped children could benefit from the greater resources and range and diversity of subjects and staff available in the ordinary school. Indeed the system of integration outlined here offers the only viable model, consonant with other objectives, for providing visually handicapped children with a fully comprehensive secondary education with direct access to higher education.

Is this practical? Many would say not, but there has been quite sufficient experience of integrating both blind and partially sighted children into ordinary schools both here and abroad to put it beyond doubt that it is entirely practical *so long as the necessary arrangements are made for providing within the ordinary school itself the specialist teaching and support which visually handicapped children clearly need.* The National

Federation of the Blind and Association of Blind and Partially
Sighted Teachers and Students (1973, 1977, 1980 and 1982)
have devoted extensive study to the practical aspects of
implementing a system of integrated special education for the
visually handicapped, and the next section outlines their
proposals in the context of the total range of provision required
for visually handicapped children generally.

The main features of a system of special education for the visually handicapped

Special education for the visually handicapped, like special
education generally, should aim to make available a range,
continuum or diversity of provision. Only thus can the much
talked-of individualization of provision be achieved or
anything like a real choice provided. To comprehend the
variety of needs evident among the visually handicapped
school population, three main types of provision need to be
made: for the seriously additionally handicapped, provision in
residential special schools; at the other end of the scale, for
those with comparatively mild visual handicaps, peripatetic
support in the local ordinary school; for those in between, the
educationally blind and those more seriously partially sighted,
as already indicated, a network of resource centres needs to be
established in selected ordinary schools throughout the
country.

The National Federation of the Blind and Association of
Blind and Partially Sighted Teachers and Students (1982) have
summarized the function, characteristics and resource
requirements of such centres as follows:

1 The centres should provide specialist teaching in the skills
  required by visually handicapped pupils, and also back-up
  support, materials and advice for those pupils and the
  members of staff who will teach them in the ordinary classes
  of the school. In particular, after initially concentrating on
  the teaching of special skills within the resource centre,
  particularly in the early years at primary level, the objective
  would be to promote the progressive integration of each

blind or partially sighted child into the ordinary classes of the school.

2 Each resource centre would provide for both blind and partially sighted children together, as recommended by the Vernon Committee, and cater for up to 5–10 blind and 10–20 partially sighted children.

3 Each resource centre would occupy about four or five small rooms at the heart of the ordinary school, and would be staffed by specially trained teachers, together with non-teaching assistants. The staffing ratios would be of the order of, in a primary school, one teacher for every five or part of five blind pupils, and one teacher for every ten or part of ten partially sighted pupils, plus one non-teaching assistant for every two teachers in the resource centre; in a secondary school, two teachers for the first 15 pupils, whether blind or partially sighted, plus one teacher for every 15 or part of 15 thereafter, plus one non-teaching assistant for every teacher.

4 Each centre would also have all the necessary equipment and materials, including books and materials in braille and large print, and the resources to produce and duplicate them, plus tape-recording equipment, aids to low vision, mobility aids, and so on.

Although the schools in which resource centres are established should be very carefully selected, in particular for their all-round quality of educational provision, motivation towards the integration scheme and location, they would not need as a rule to be specially adapted in their physical structure. Visually handicapped children have no difficulty in coping physically in special schools that have not been specially adapted for them in any way; and given that one of the functions of the resource centre would be to provide or secure mobility training and aids, this should not present any particular problem in the ordinary school either. Nor should there be any great difficulty in making available in the ordinary school whatever in the way of resources is currently made available in special schools. Indeed the ordinary school will probably have a larger stock of 'general' resources from which the visually handicapped child will be able to benefit. Provided, too, that specialist teaching assistance is made available for the visually handicapped children as indicated above, there should be no problem over providing ordinary class teachers with the back-up support, guidance and advice which they will need in order to be able to cope with visually handicapped children in their classes. Home–school transport services would need to be considerably geared up to meet the needs of visually handicapped children attending ordinary schools with a resource centre, but savings on the cost of sending children away to residential special schools out-county would more than offset the cost of this.

In areas with a particularly small and far-flung visually handicapped population, peripatetic support in local schools may be the only alternative to boarding special education. It is not as good as support from a resource centre within the school, but it operates satisfactorily in sparsely populated parts of the United States, and is generally to be preferred to boarding special education.

If the official 'blind education system' is afflicted by so many problems, and an alternative blueprint without such drawbacks not only lies ready to hand but has actually been implemented successfully in many parts of the world, why should the 'blind education system', with all its difficulties, have displayed such resilience, and the alternative special educational strategy been taken up in so few quarters here? The answer to this question must at least in part lie with the institutional resistance and ideological factors to which I now turn.

Institutional resistance

It is sometimes suggested that if integration has such a compelling logic for the official 'blind education system', nothing much needs to be done in order to bring it about. But if this is not actually disingenuous, it is extremely politically naive. As Tony Booth (1981) has pointed out, the special education system has a momentum of its own. So long as special schools continue to exist and we continue to carry on running them, there will be places to be filled and people with an interest in filling them. At a time when space is at a discount, even single individuals can make a difference to viability. There will be pressure to retain the less handicapped within the system as a leaven for the other children and the staff. We can soon end up reaching the point where the children are meeting the needs of the institutions instead of the other way about. At the very least, the forces of inertia tell heavily in favour of the special school sector. A major redeployment of resources requires planning, effort, commitment and will. People have to change their established practices and modes of working. How much simpler just to carry on operating the well-tried procedures! As Booth (1982) has said:

> There are practical problems in integrating some handicapped children in some parts of the country. But often the practical difficulties have more to do with the reorganisation of jobs and occupational aspirations, with the reallocation of money and resources, than with the needs of children. This inertia within the system is an important human issue, and any change requires skill, sense and sensitivity. (Booth 1981, p.308)

These points are well illustrated by the particular problem posed by the special grammar schools for the blind run by the Royal National Institute for the Blind for boys and girls respectively at Worcester and Chorleywood. In order to enhance their effectiveness and assure their viability, the Institute is presently seeking to merge the two schools, either on one of the existing sites, or on a third site altogether, possibly in conjunction with another school for the blind. Some special schools for visually handicapped children with serious additional handicaps will continue to be needed, but if the integration is going to take place on any scale at all among the blind, the children who have typically gone to Worcester and Chorleywood in the past will be prime candidates for making the transition. Thus the two schools present a key impediment to structural reorganization. At a time when one is trying to redeploy resources for special education towards the ordinary school sector, it makes no sense to be making a major new investment in the special school sector, such as the reconstitution of Worcester and Chorleywood would unquestionably represent. The creaming off of all the most suitable candidates would throw up a stumbling block to the development of properly designed projects for supporting the integration of blind children into ordinary schools at a local level of the kind discussed above. With all the institutional pressures that inevitably exist to fill special school places once they have been created, rather than going to the considerable trouble of developing support systems in ordinary schools of their own, it would be a natural temptation for local education authorities simply to send blind children to the residential schools where they know that provision has traditionally been made for them. Furthermore, given the present very general lack of proper provision for visually handicapped children in ordinary schools, those with responsibility for advising on placement have little alternative but to steer children towards this special school sector.

To the extent that the merger of Worcester and Chorleywood does not have the consequences feared above, and local schemes of integration do begin to blossom, then by contrast it will tend to lead to a wasteful over-provision of special school places. If the trend towards integration gathers pace, there would in fact be serious danger of creating a costly white elephant if the residential sector of secondary education for the blind was continued in the manner proposed. We have already seen that the number of blind children of secondary school age may be as low as 350 by the end of the decade. As many as a third of these could require the very special provision reserved for those with serious additional handicaps, and not all the rest will be of Worcester–Chorleywood standard. A merged selective school providing 150 places, i.e. the size of the two existing schools combined, would thus be bound either to 'scoop the pool' or end up as a half-empty mausoleum. Instead of attempting to shore up an honourable but essentially outmoded tradition, the RNIB would be better putting its resources into helping to promote good schemes of integration at local level.

Ideological factors

Special education, like most mysteries, is too important to be left to the professionals – they mystify things too much. Certainly the sort of institutional resistance just described is powerfully buttressed by a series of plausible misconceptions and misrepresentations that may be said to amount to an ideology of special education. The fact that much of this rests on an extremely insecure foundation of confusion and distortion is not to the point. The power of an ideology has much more to do with its value in supporting a particular view of the world than with the rationality of its specific propositions. A fuller account of these can be found in Low (1981). Space permits only the following summary here:

1 The essential slipperyness of the notion of integration, its convenient ability to mean all things to all men, make it a veritable godsend to the practitioners of mystification. Integration is portrayed as treating everyone, handicapped and unhandicapped alike, exactly the same. The opponents of integration are thus enabled to argue that integration is incompatible with providing the kind of special help that handicapped children clearly need. But such an antithesis is wholly false. As we have seen, responsible advocates of integration for the visually handicapped are at considerable pains to specify how the necessary help can be made available. For them, 'integration' essentially means 'supported integration'. The only difference that separates them from their critics is their concern to see help mobilized in the ordinary school at the heart instead of on the periphery of the community.

2 We have already remarked the tendency to talk of anything other than education in a special school for the visually handicapped as integration, regardless of the level of support provided. From there it is but a short step to pointing to the children who have not fared well in ordinary schools that did not have properly constituted resource centres, and who have perhaps had to move into the special school sector, as the 'casualties' or 'failures' of integration. But as will be clear, it would be quite wrong to write off the whole idea of integration in this way, given the almost total absence of properly supported schemes of integration in this country at the present time.

3 It is often said that the mere fact of being educated in an ordinary school does not of itself constitute integration. The same point is made another way when people insist that it is the quality of provision that counts, not where it is made. But other things being equal, the ordinary school must be better as a base for integration than the special school. Though presence in an ordinary school may not be a sufficient condition of full integration, it is certainly a necessary one. The point was perhaps put most sharply for the visually handicapped by the Vernon Committee (DES 1972, para. 5.30):

> We are deeply impressed by the argument that, if visually handicapped children are to be fitted through their education to live in the world with sighted people, the best way for them to acquire the necessary ability and confidence is to mix as freely as possible with sighted children during their schooldays. Social events arranged with neighbouring sighted schools may help a little, but contacts tend to be artificial or at least superficial; in order to get to know sighted children and to feel at home with them, a visually handicapped child needs to be in the same school as they are.

4 Finally, calls for integration are frequently presented as too 'dogmatic', 'doctrinaire' or 'extreme'. Provision needs to be made, it is said, not according to some abstract principle, but according to the differing needs of each individual child. Those who can benefit from integration should certainly be integrated, but for those who need the sheltering care of the special school, this option should still be retained. All this sounds eminently reasonable, but again it caricatures the integrationists' position. For they, no less than their segregationist critics, recognize the need for a properly individualized range of provision, not excluding placement in a special school in cases of appropriate severity. But in a situation where the special school sector has a virtual monopoly, this argument points entirely in the direction of extending systems of support within the framework of the ordinary school.

The need for a planned approach

There needs to be planning for supported integration. It is not enough simply to impose, as the 1981 Education Act does, a general obligation to integrate, subject to considerations of educational suitability and efficiency. Without establishing any mechanism for ensuring that the support necessary to make integration a practical proposition is made available in ordinary schools, nothing very much is likely to happen. Given the current absence of facilities in ordinary schools for children with special needs, the educational criteria are seldom likely to be met. In these circumstances, the possibilities of integration will simply be bounded by the limitations inherent in existing arrangements.

The Act is far too individualistic in its approach. It imposes certain obligations to provide the necessary support if a handicapped child should happen to turn up in an ordinary school. But the crucial point is that without the making of systematic arrangements that might make this more likely to happen in the first place, the arrival of a handicapped child in an ordinary school will be a happy accident at best, but will more probably be ruled out altogether by the inadequacy of existing provision.

Imagine the situation in concrete terms: in the face of a specific request to integrate, one of two things must necessarily occur – either integration will not be attempted for want of the necessary support, or it will, but with disastrous results for the same reason. Many authorities profess a commitment to integration in principle, but demonstrate little awareness of the implications of such a commitment in practice. That being so, the most likely response will probably be simply to drift along with the existing pattern of special schools by sending children away *faute de mieux*. If this is to be avoided, there needs to be a planned development at local authority level of the necessary systems for meeting special educational needs in ordinary schools.

What should be the locus of planning? Every LEA should have a plan, but should it always be a plan for making the necessary provision itself? If the optimum number of resource centres for visually handicapped children is only some 40 or 50 each at primary and secondary level, the answer to this question would seem to be 'no', indicating the desirability of a degree of regional planning; each region should probably have a specialist adviser on the visually handicapped. But the outcome of regional planning has, as we have seen, been disappointing. Nor do local education authorities seem very good at co-operating with one another at subregional level. In these circumstances, pinpointing a number of key authorities, strategic in terms of their size and location, and attempting to persuade them to implement a plan for integration, would seem to afford the best prospect of advance. There is some evidence to suggest that neighbouring authorities would then be more than happy to ride on the back of such a plan, just as they do now on the backs of the special schools. In this way the original authority could also probably be assured of recouping a fair proportion of its costs.

A problem that authorities often come up with is that of the small number of visually handicapped children in relation to the total school population, or even to that of children with other types of handicap. Would it be acceptable, they often ask, to achieve economies of scale by setting up support units for the visually handicapped in conjunction with units for children suffering from different types of handicap? To this, the answer seems fairly clearly to be that it is certainly acceptable to establish units for children suffering from more than one type of handicap in a single school. But separate units need to be established, and there probably should not be too many of them – probably not more than a couple in fact – if handicap is not to impose a disproportionate burden on the school and stretch the staff beyond its limit. There is clearly a limit to the range of problems that any given staff can be expected to deal with. At all events, the most important point is that a special support unit must specialize in the distinct problems that are undeniably still thrown up by at least some of the traditional categories of handicap. Of these, the visually handicapped are certainly one.

Conclusion

The conception of integration advanced in this chapter represents an essentially moderate form of the proposal, viz., one of 'making ordinary schools special' – of a substantial redeployment of resources from the special to the ordinary school sector – but on a selective basis, to selected 'centres of excellence' specializing to some degree in the education of the visually handicapped. Such a model would not commend itself to all integrationists, some of whom, it seems, rightly seeing integration as a logical extension of the comprehensive principle, would regard even this as subjecting the children concerned to too much invidious differentiation, and would prefer to see all schools being able to respond sympathetically to the individual needs of all types of children.

Integration is not an all or nothing matter. The situation is both fluid and dynamic. A few pioneering ventures in supported integration have begun to be undertaken, but the special school system is under pressure and will unquestionably try to fight back. Things could well go either way. Realistically, one cannot effect a total transformation, even of a subsystem such as the education system, all at once. I prefer a more dialectical approach. The tender shoots of new integration schemes that have already put down their roots need nurturing and extending. That way we can hope to gain some purchase on the education system that could pave the way for more far-reaching developments later on. By attempting everything at once we could well fail.

3
Creating Integration Policy

TONY BOOTH

Introduction

I shall start this chapter by describing four attempts to increase the participation of children with 'special' needs within ordinary comprehensive primary and secondary schools. I shall then consider the implications of these schemes for the creation of a national policy for integrating special education. I shall argue that integration has to be created by people who are often working against the tide of events and that the efforts of individuals have to be co-ordinated by policy directives at both national and LEA levels. I shall examine some of the changes in the approach to policy-making that must take place if integration is to be achieved and ask to what extent the 1981 Act can be part of such a process. I shall suggest that policy initiatives should be informed by a coherent philosophy as well as a deep knowledge about current practice and that they require a new style of educational leadership matched by a devolution of decision-making to schools and their communities. I shall end the chapter by indicating some of the structures LEAs might establish if they are to create a flow towards an integrated education system.

The form that eduational policy takes will vary with regional differences in education. In Northern Ireland 'integration' means Protestant and Catholic children learning together. I visited the only 'integrated' primary school in Belfast which happens to be an ESN(M) school. Secondary education in Northern Ireland is selective and it is simply not possible to link the issue of the integration of the handicapped, in any practical way, to the development of comprehensive education there. In

Scotland the scale of the system and degree of informal centralization of education makes it more like Norway in some respects than England. Any specific plan for integration has to take the local provision, resources, expertise and needs as its starting points.

Putting integration into practice

The four examples of 'integration' schemes I have chosen illustrate the variety of issues involved in establishing integration policy. They include blind and partially sighted children, children with mental handicaps, an attempt to include children from remedial groups into the mainstream of school life and also efforts to adjust the curriculum and methods of teaching within secondary schools so that all children receive an appropriate education. The examples are arranged in a progression from school-based changes through LEA initiatives to national developments for 'pupils with learning difficulties' in Scotland.

A resource area for blind and partially sighted children
The development of unit provision for blind and partially sighted children attached to an ordinary school described by Hegarty and Pocklington (1981a) was initiated by a senior educational administrator. But changes within schools depend on the active agreement of those with the power to implement them and the role of the headteacher is crucial. When these children were first introduced to the school their specialist teacher-in-charge felt that they should be retained, by and large, as a separate group for their education with some degree of social mixing. The headteacher however was determined that they should become an integral part of the school, in which team teaching and vertical grouping had already prepared the ground for catering for different educational needs within the same teaching area. She eventually turned the 'unit' into a resource area, and attached the children to registration groups in the main school. She moved her room and the secretary's office into what had been the administration rooms for the unit and then turned the entrance to the resource area into the main

entrance to the school. In this way she placed the blind and partially sighted children at the centre of the life of the school both educationally and geographically.

Developing remedial education in a comprehensive school
In some schools the distribution of power between those advocating and opposing change may be more finely balanced and the struggle over whose views will predominate may be characterized by plots and counterplots. Chalkway School (Booth and Flynn 1982) had contained two separate class groups designated as 'remedial' and 'near remedial'. The remedial group were taught as a class group for all subjects except maths, when they joined the setting system of the rest of the school. The 'near remedial' group joined the setting system for all setted subjects except French. The head of the remedial department, who was not included in meetings of 'senior staff', gained the support of one of the two deputy heads and together with a couple of other members of staff devised a plan for moving from separate class provision to a system of support by withdrawal from mixed-ability classes. In the first instance they proposed the abolition of the 'near remedial group' and gained the acceptance of the idea in the senior staff committee. However over the summer break the plans were changed unilaterally by staff who disagreed with the changes and the school timetable still designated a group of pupils to miss French and be taught as the 'possible-near-remedials'. When the remedial staff returned they once more formed a group, gained the support of the head of French and managed to implement their original plan. They set about devising a plan for abolishing remedial groups in the following year.

Provision for mentally handicapped children in Bromley
If an LEA were attempting to act on a principle of integration one might expect them to put integration schemes into operation, after advisers and administrators had sought to discover how such schemes were effectively organized in other parts of the country. That integration initiatives have not spread from one LEA to another tells us something about LEA commitment to integration policy, but the failure of integration to expand *within* those authorities that have been

successfully including handicapped pupils for many years can be even more revealing.

In the London Borough of Bromley mentally handicapped children have been educated within units in ordinary schools since 1971 when such children came within the responsibility of the education system. The classes work well, the children appear to receive an effective education, and they and their parents have the additional benefits of integration. They have been accepted by other children and the parents of the non-handicapped, which was especially evident when the parents of the non-handicapped children raised £10,000 in order to refurbish a unit at one school after administrators had suggested that the group be moved to newer accommodation at another school. But if the classes were working well in the estimation of LEA officials, why hadn't this scheme been extended into the junior or secondary stage or broadened to include other groups of handicapped children?

The study by the National Foundation for Education Research on the Bromley classes suggests that mentally handicapped 3–8-year-olds are in normal schools to permit a lengthy period of assessment before a 'final' decision is taken about appropriate placement (Hegarty and Pocklington 1982). I had suspected that failure to extend the classes into junior schools and beyond was the result of a conflict between two sides in the LEA, with the segregationists regaining the upper hand. After talking with the retired assistant education officer who had had major responsibilities for setting up the classes, a more complex story emerged. Some of the conflicting tendencies to integrate and segregate were mediated by the same person.

The assistant education officer argued that it had been his proposals to the education committee that had established the special classes and that there had been little opposition to the plan. He thought that once administrators had reached a position of trust with their education committee, proposals were usually ratified without detailed discussion of philosophies. There had been little opposition from his colleagues either. Before 1971 the training centre, which had places for 80 children, contained 120. There was no provision for the under-fives and several older children were at home. There was an urgent need to find additional school places.

The assistant education officer's decision to create special classes in the infant schools was influenced by opinions from a number of directions. There was considerable pressure by the Bromley Society for Mentally Handicapped Children, a vociferous and well-organized group who pressed strongly for integration. Their efforts were given added weight because they followed a successful campaign by the local society for the deaf who had been outraged at the total lack of provision for deaf children in Bromley. He discussed the ideas with people from the Campaign for Mental Handicap and he drew on the work of Tizard (1972), which had implied that mentally handicapped children could respond well to an environment like that of a good infant school.

The provision was therefore started with groups of mentally handicapped children placed in the 'best' infant schools in middle-class areas of the borough. The authority had also suspected that they might get adverse reactions from other children, or their parents, in priority areas. But when a group was placed in a school in such an area the anticipated difficulties did not occur. They were surprised at how readily the children were accepted.

The assistant education officer gave two main reasons for the failure to extend provision to the junior age range. The junior schools in the area did not contain heads with the same interest in working with mentally handicapped children. But the most important reason was that he had miscalculated the demand for provision. At the same time as he was establishing the special classes he had pressed through committee plans for the building of a new ESN(S) school. It was built for 100 children but when it opened it had only 12 pupils. Once it had been built the new school created pressures of its own. Its existence had to be justified. The only infant and junior school to have groups of mentally handicapped children had one group who were profoundly handicapped. This group was moved across to the new special school to make the numbers more respectable and gradually its numbers built up to a reasonable level. While he recognized that the new school was good as a special school, he did think that a mistake had been made.

Pupils with learning difficulties in Scotland
The events in Bromley, as those at Chalkway School, illustrate
the fragile nature of reforms that are not tied to a coherent
LEA plan or philosophy. These can be contrasted with some
aspects of the changes that have been taking place in the
education of pupils with learning diffculties in Scotland (see
Booth 1983).In 1978 the Scottish HMI produced a progress
report on the education of pupils with learning difficulties in
ordinary schools (SED 1978). It was based on a survey of
existing remedial provision in Scotland and was highly critical
of the ordinary school curriculum, which promoted failure,
and a system of remedial education based on a limited, basic
skills curriculum provided in separate classes or withdrawal
groups.

The report attempted to summarize, stimulate and extend
good practice. It called for all teachers to take responsibility for
the learning difficulties of children who might comprise up to
50 per cent of the school population, for the extension of
mixed-ability teaching, for the minimum withdrawal of pupils
and the development of team teaching, for assessment related
to the abilities of pupils, for as many curriculum options for the
least as the most able, and for particular attention to be paid to
transfer between primary and secondary schooling. Although
the head was to take overall responsibility for pupils with
learning difficulties in her school, the major responsibility for
implementing these changes was to rest with remedial
specialists. One adviser in English was prompted to ask:

> Where are they all? The ordinary-looking teachers who
> will disappear into the remedial base, spin round and
> emerge from the ball of light, garishly costumed, thighs
> bared, all set to be tutors, monitors, cooperative partners,
> diagnosticians, healers, tacticians, consultants and
> experts in language and learning? Where is wonder-
> teacher, without whose timely intervention learning
> difficulties will gain control of the world? (Lamont 1981,
> p.6)

But the impact of the report also relied heavily on the
closeness of the relationship between the Scottish HMI and

LEA administration. A senior administrator in each authority was to have overall responsibility for pushing through the reforms. In Fife a depute director of education said, 'instead of debating its contents we decided to work out how to do something about it.' They set annual targets and established curriculum committees in the schools. By August 1981 they abolished all separate remedial classes and by August 1982 aimed to reduce the number of different teachers for first-year pupils in secondary schools, to introduce block timetabling and to increase the emphasis on project work.

In Grampian, which was one of the areas on which the HMI report had been based, the depute director for secondary education had the job of co-ordinating developments in remedial provision. In an interview he made it clear that it was part of his job to initiate and guide a region-wide policy:

> I have no doubt that it's my job as an official to make recommendations to the education committee after appropriate consultation and then produce broad policy guidelines. Remedial education is a good example. Within certain guidelines you are free to exercise your own professional judgement but there are certain things you must not do, you must not have a separate class for remedial youngsters. (Booth 1983, p.42)

The Grampian schools were organized into groups with a single secondary school and its feeder primaries. A principal remedial teacher was attached to each secondary school with responsibility for a group of remedial staff some of whom worked as 'float teachers' in both secondary and primary schools. The number of remedial teachers in the area was expanded from 160 to 260, and these were allocated to the schools according to need. The posts were taken out of the reckoning for potential educational cuts.

The two major roles of this new breed of remedial specialist are firstly to act as consultants to other members of staff on children's learning difficulties, the development of curriculum materials and on appropriate teaching strategies, and secondly to work alongside subject specialists and primary class teachers in the ordinary classroom. The credibility of the remedial teachers to act as consultants rests on the abilities they display in team teaching. A diploma in the teaching of pupils with learning difficulties is being developed nationally in an attempt to reinforcc the expertise the new roles require.

It is always easier to make changes in formal structures than in relationships between people or in teaching content and methods. Some teachers have found it extremely difficult to work alongside another member of staff and Ferguson and Adams (1982) have documented some of the difficulties that arose:

> One class teacher described remedial teachers as 'rather ingratiating – embarrassed by their position. They have an urge to justify their existence'. Another commented testily 'she [the remedial teacher] is inclined to take over the whole class. Suddenly she's in the middle directing the class if I go out for a minute.' (Ferguson and Adams 1982, p.27)

In other cases the co-operation has worked well and has formed an effective means of in-service education for both participants. Remedial education is now taking place in science, cookery, maths and French as well as English. One remedial teacher remarked on her involvement in a science lesson:

> We really share the class teaching; we are shoulder to shoulder as class teachers. . . . Initially I was very wary but now it's so relaxed that I can intervene at any point. If I feel they haven't understood something I pick it up and put it across in a different way. . . . (Booth 1983, p.46)

The science specialist with whom she worked found the joint teaching of tremendous benefit, commenting on the advantages of individual attention, teacher continuity and the sharing of discipline and planning. But how one reacts to the difficulties that arise as an inevitable consequence of change in people's lives depends on one's assumptions. If the change is desired then one asks: How can the problems be overcome? If the change is deplored then difficulties become evidence of policy failure.

Some implications of practice for policy-making

Left to themselves, then, schools often have not developed and sometimes cannot develop plans for integration. Although there are several individual schools outside Scotland where remedial education is given a broad and powerful role, in the absence of LEA support those wishing to innovate expend much of their energy getting schemes off the ground and then preserving them. In hierarchically structured schools change requires the support of senior members of staff and depends largely on the decision of the headteacher. This decision may be easily subverted by staff changes, the emergence of new priorities and the shifting balance of power. Developments involving more than one school require the initiative or support of a powerful official within the LEA. But LEAs are big places and unless a development is part of an LEA-wide plan it may be in competition with other provision or practices in the LEA. The support service described by Neville Hallmark in chapter 10 coexists with conventional ESN(M) schools.

The assistant education officer's story in Bromley illustrates some of the problems in trying to reverse a trend in local education policies by individual efforts in one area of education. Ways of thinking become institutionalized, familiar solutions are repeated and become tied to administrative departments and budgets. These tendencies within an LEA may be too dominant to be deflected by the efforts of one person or of a single group of parents whose pressure is deflated once they gain some measure of success for their own children. The fact that in Bromley the contradictory forces were propelled by the same person only appears startling because we are not used to people exhibiting their contradictions in public. A very similar story must exist in virtually every local education authority in the country where piecemeal integration and piecemeal segregation alternate as the solution to meeting the special needs of children.

A number of people have reacted very defensively to accounts of integration schemes in Bromley claiming that they do not give full credit to the excellent work taking place in the ESN(S) schools there. But that reaction only highlights the problems associated with redirecting educational policy.

Integration requires change. It creates discomfort and involves a considerable challenge to those whose careers, work and social relationships reinforce a segregated system.

There are the beginnings of coherent national and regional policy changes for 'pupils with learning difficulties' in Scotland. Whether or not traditional practices will reassert themselves depends on the extent to which the initial effort can be sustained and institutionalized in national training courses, in-service training and school tradition. I suspect too that they will have to be supported by an openly acknowledged educational philosophy which can be drawn on to justify and initiate day-to-day practice, and it is in this respect that the developments may be weakest.

There is no explicit connection between the Scottish policy developments and an overall philosophy of integration although one may emerge. The depute director in Grampian claimed that primary and secondary schools were reducing their referrals to special schools because of the support available within their own schools. But in 1981 the Scottish HMI issued a further report on the curriculum for 'mildly mentally handicapped' pupils of secondary school age offered in special schools (SED 1981). Although the report is critical of existing provision the special school is still described as the appropriate place for the education of these children.

One might argue, too, that the Scottish initiatives stretch the definition of 'learning difficulties' beyond sense. Can 50 per cent of pupils be said to have 'learning difficulties' and be 'in need of remedial education'? In practice the remedy is clear; it is schools rather than children to whom remedial education is to be applied and the number of ailing curricula may approach 100 per cent. It is a reform of comprehensive education rather than an increase in special provision that is seen as the appropriate step. But perhaps, then, the remedial specialist should be seen as a support teacher for a comprehensive differentiated curriculum and the learning difficulties diploma should be explicitly about the creation, of *schools for all*.

Creating a national integration policy

The developments in Scotland represent an approach to

policy-making that is quite foreign to LEA administrators and teachers in the rest of the United Kingdom. The idea that an LEA should devise, circulate and implement a regional plan might even send shivers up and down the spines of a few of them. According to one American observer special education in the United Kingdom is 'almost exclusively the province of specialists, an institutional marginal service, isolated from ordinary schools and managed by a specialist group . . . orders are rare and government by circular the norm. The system is perceived by its participants as depending on hint and signal, consultation and suggestion' (Kirp 1982). Unlike in the United States where consumers led the changes in special education policy by challenging in the courts the unconstitutional nature of the education given to their children, policy developments in the United Kingdom have depended on the assumed benevolence of professional groups. If integration is to occur in a widespread or thoroughgoing way then we shall need to rethink our approaches to policy-making.

Rhetoric and reality
The development of an integration policy has been impeded by a belief that it can be expected to happen as part of a natural evolution in attitudes towards the handicapped. Such a view is supported by an apparently similar progression in several developed nations. After a period of passive or active exclusion of the handicapped from education, separate facilities were established with a measure of positive discrimination. This expansion was followed by reforming interest and then legislation curtailing the growth of segregated special schooling and initiating the inclusion of handicapped children in ordinary schools. A reading of Pritchard's (1963) history of special education would suggest that such 'progress' was ensured by the benevolence of history. But a closer examination of national practices makes such a simple view difficult to maintain. Changes typically involve considerable conflict. They are rarely as widespread or complete as they might at first seem and there are several national exceptions to the rule.

In the United Kingdom, government documents, reports and legislation have indicated that they were endorsing a trend towards integration. Since 1954, at the latest, official government documents have espoused the virtues of the integration of 'handicapped children'. Ministry of Education Circular 26 said that 'no handicapped child should be sent to a special school who can satisfactorily be educated in an ordinary school.' By the 1970s such documents were not only advocating the principle but were claiming that it was being given practical effect. A DES booklet issued in 1974 argued that 'the extent to which this [i.e. integration] is already taking place is perhaps not commonly realized' (DES 1974, p.3). The Warnock Report claimed to offer 'proof that segregation is diminishing' (DES 1978, p.99). Yet from the fifties to the eighties there has been a dramatic growth in all forms of segregated provision, both in terms of special schools and special units and classes outside as well as within ordinary schools. By the end of the seventies this growth had slowed but there was no evidence of a drop in the *proportion* of children excluded from ordinary schools and classrooms though falling rolls were affecting all sectors of education. These trends and the reasons for them and for official mystifications were analysed in another article (Booth 1981) and it appeared that official documents were not only misleading but also concealed the existence of a widespread desire to segregate increasing numbers of children.

The national trends did not apply to all groups of children; there was a tendency for the proportion of children in special schools for sight difficulties to reduce, though Colin Low relates this to a drop in prevalence (see chapter 2). Any set of national statistics also conceals opposing trends in different regions. But the overall trend was in the opposite direction and when this was coupled with the dramatic growth in off-site unit provision, particularly for children regarded as 'disruptive', the drive towards segregation was even more evident. The most recently available figures (DES 1981) do reveal a slight overall drop from the previous year in the proportion of children in special schools but to what extent such a trend will persist remains to be seen.

An active policy for change
Integration cannot happen by itself. We have an educational

system too rooted in a philosophy of selection to expect a consensus shift in educational practice. Yet the production of a coherent change in educational thinking goes against strong traditions for *laissez-faire* policy-making in LEAs, particularly in England and Wales. Policy-making in which little attempt is made to harmonize diverse and competing forces can be called 'drift'.

Active educational policy-making involves a deliberate attempt to control educational practice informed by a rational and coherent philosophy which sustains the spirit of new policies through changing economic and political circumstances. The creation of an active policy depends on power and knowledge. In order to reshape present special educational practice we have to have the power to implement change but we also require a deep knowledge of current practice at all levels of the system, as well as the forces that sustain and control it.

The Warnock Report has been widely viewed as giving general support to integration. LEA officials and others suggest, commonly, that integration plans are 'in line with Warnock'. Yet the report seemed to cloud the integration issue, by misinterpreting trends in the placement of handicapped children. It failed to link integration to reforms of comprehensive, primary and secondary schools and hence did not elaborate on the forms of organization, teaching and curricula that might be required in the integrated school. But there also seemed to be an element of deliberate obscurity. As Mrs Warnock herself remarked: 'People have said we fudged the issue of integration, but we fudged it as a matter of policy' (*Times Educational Supplement*, 25 May 1978).

The Warnock Report was right to point out the conceptual confusion in maintaining rigid divisions between special, remedial and ordinary education, but it did not anticipate and analyse the resistance to change within the education system. In some schools where there are attempts to integrate children from ESN(M) schools, separate remedial departments persist with their own pupils and staff. Teachers, parents and support professionals have become accustomed to assuming the rationality of a system which divided the 'ESN(M) child' from the ordinarily slow and the ordinarily naughty and unhappy from the 'maladjusted'. The very existence of a career progression which involves increasing specialization and expertise in relation to children identified as having problems must ensure some interest in maintaining existing distinctions. The forces that created a separate special educational system are not going to be undone simply by displaying the logical faults in the arguments that sustain them.

One of the hazards of policy-making is that those with the knowledge often have little power and the powerful may be too far removed from practice to devise sensible strategies. The development of a national integration policy would involve an increase in direction from central government and LEA administration. But effective policy-making depends, too, on a narrowing of the gap between policy-makers and practitioners. I was particularly struck by the willingness of LEA administration in Scotland to become intimately involved in the creation of regional policy as well as in its day-to-day implementation. As one depute director remarked in an interview, 'I suppose fundamentally I'm classified as "an educational administrator"; in my book the emphasis is on the first word, not the second. The second is a necessary evil.' (Booth 1983, p.42)

In framing special education law in the United States legislators failed to examine in sufficient detail the effect it would have on the working patterns of teachers and support professionals (see Booth 1982c). The transformation of policy to fit into the day-to-day lives of practitioners has led to the latter being dubbed 'street level bureaucrats' (Weatherley and Lipsky 1981). But it is not sufficient for a change to be possible to avoid the subversion of a centrally initiated policy.

Practitioners have to create the space in their own lives to make the changes, and they have to agree to make them. Such a contract might best be achieved by the close involvement of the consumers of policy in its conception. By its nature integration policy depends for its implementation on the involvement of teachers and students and families. In closing the gap between policy-makers, teachers, children and their families an integration policy demands that all the other participants in special education should move towards an understanding of the needs, interests and rights of pupils and their families.

Integration policy and the 1981 Act

Can the 1981 Act contribute towards an active integration policy? It was based on an assumption that it was giving the process of integration an encouraging nod rather than helping to define, initiate and co-ordinate a process that was often in opposition to existing trends. It contained a formula for the inclusion of handicapped children in ordinary schools which continues an ambiguity of the Warnock Report. All children are to be in ordinary schools except those for whom it is not practically feasible or interferes with the education of other children or is not financially viable. Are these exceptions to be greater or fewer in number than those currently educated in special schools?

The Act was framed, too, within a strong tradition in the United Kingdom, amounting to a national slogan, for local autonomy. In such circumstances the purpose of legislation may be obscured. I have heard the Act called a piece of enabling legislation. Yet if it enables LEAs to devise opposing policies, what is it for? All new law, if it means anything, imposes some new degree of conformity, some restriction in freedom, at least for some people. The justification of new law is that it also produces an increase in freedom, possibly for other people.

As it stands the 1981 Act appears to legitimate the production of educational policy by market forces. But it is still possible that a measure of coherence can be given to integration in the United Kingdom either through the regulations and circulars issued by the DES or through consumer pressure or by recognition within individual LEAs of the conditions for the effective creation of policy.

A way forward

The implementation of an integration policy requires a new approach to planning and educational administration by LEAs. It requires a commitment to a philosophy of comprehensive education and a willingness to elaborate plans and see them through. Other chapters in this book suggest some of the ways in which management structures and the roles of teachers and support professionals will have to be revised. I want to end this chapter by suggesting two preconditions for effective LEA policy development.

The production of LEA plans

The publishing of a public annual plan by each LEA would appear to be a fundamental precondition for effective policy-making that could lay any claim to inviting participation or hence have hope for serious implementation. One could expect an LEA plan to have three major elements: a detailed description of all existing special education provision both inside and outside ordinary schools; a general description of changes planned over a five-year period; and a detailed description of the change planned in the following year. Such plans should reflect the abolition of distinctions between 'remedial' and 'special' and should not omit any group of excluded pupils such as the 'disaffected'. They should link all developments in special education to the implementation of a comprehensive education system, but clearly the existence of separate plans would perpetuate a distinction between special and ordinary education and that is a paradox of moves towards integration. If a philosophy of integration gains ground then ultimately there may be no need for separate special educational plans.

The creation of policy areas

LEAs are too large effectively to permit the participation of teachers and communities in policy development and the school is too narrow a unit, partly because the needs of children must be seen as a whole as they progress through the education system and also in order to include children who may not be within ordinary schools at present. In Grampian they have grouped a single secondary school and their feeder primaries, and in Oxfordshire they are beginning moves towards a federal structure, linking a group of comprehensive schools and primary schools together. But if all the support from health, education and social services is to be linked then the policy area has to be a community of people rather than particular schools like the parish used to be in some respects or the commune is in present-day Norway. Special schools and units might be attached to policy areas and policy teams after the 'twinning' model introduced in Denmark. Such an arrangement involves a degree of administrative amalgamation with the ordinary schools and facilitates a movement of teachers and students and a sharing of expertise and curricula.

Each policy area might have a policy team formed from the schools and their community. Policy teams are being developed in parts of Oxfordshire and exist for remedial services in Grampian. There is a definite danger though that reforms with a power base in the secondary schools or any other sector of education may produce changes that are unduly influenced by current organization and curricula of that sector.

Each policy team would develop its own agenda but there are several issues which would be common to most teams:

1 curriculum and staff development in relation to children with special needs in the schools;
2 parental and community involvement in the schools;
3 co-ordinating support services for children with special needs;
4 arranging and supporting the transfer of children, staff and resources from special to ordinary schools;
5 the creation of physical access to the schools for children and adults including educational employees;
6 developing resource bases in the school.

A concluding remark

In this chapter I have attempted to answr the question: 'If we desire integration how might we achieve it?' My answer is inevitably very incomplete. It is certainly not a prediction of what may happen and contains my own balance between what I see as the formidable obstacles to change and the need to provide information and discuss strategies if a desired trend is to be set in motion. Even with the best will the pattern of special educational provision can only reflect the talents, limitations and commitments of the people who are the system. Yet it is only through the co-ordination and expression of particular wills that integration can begin to be achieved.

4

The Management of Integration: the Oxfordshire Experience

NEVILLE JONES

Introduction

The aim of integration is to enable children with special needs to maximize their opportunities, potential and personal fulfilment in their family life, in school and in the wider community. The assumption of integrationists is that this cannot occur while children, through no choice of their own, are excluded from part of community life. What is described below is an account of the development of some of the ideas and practices of integration within a local education authority and the changes that this can entail when integration is interpreted, in two ways. First, there is the process of returning to mainstream schools those children who have been streamed out of ordinary schools and placed in special schools. Here the underlying principle is that of 'normalizing' children's educational experiences and is linked to notions of 'rehabilitation'.

Secondly, there is the notion of integration which is linked to a view of wholeness. Education has to be seen as a response to the needs of complete people rather than intellects or disabilities. But the notion of a 'whole' child embodied in much of the thinking behind the recommendations of the Warnock Committee has to find a further reflection in the concept of the 'whole' school. Such a view prompts the question: what kind of places would 'ordinary schools' have to become if segregation ceased to be seen as the only viable way of managing the special needs of children?

At the moment ordinary schools are structured on an assumption that children with extreme needs, whether these are related to the less able, the physically disabled, or the behaviourally disturbing, receive their education out of normal classes and often out of mainstream education altogether. An effective educational response to children at the extremes of need requires more than tolerance, more than special classes and units. It requires a restructuring of the 'normal' system as this relates to teacher skills, attitudes towards disability, pupil–teacher ratios, curriculum expectations, types of additional support, and so forth.

In the view of one comprehensive head, 'the Warnock Report had quietly unleashed a revolution which is of much greater consequence to the educational process than all the structural transmogrifications which over the past two decades we have described as comprehensive education' (Sayer 1981). If discussions of integration imply a revolution in thinking about the way we respond to those who have special needs, it is not in the way we teach such children in special schools, but in the way that ordinary schools will be required to organize themselves so that all children with or without special needs can participate as fully as possible. Integration affects all who work in and manage and consume the education service: administrators, advisers, support services, teachers, governors, parents and children.

An evolving pattern?

The developments within Oxfordshire from 1970 to 1980 did not come about because there was an overall strategy enshrined in a policy document. In fact it is doubtful whether there are half a dozen local education authorities in Britain where the chief education officer could put his hand into his desk and withdraw such a document that in any way matches the need for comprehensive planning and change. Change tends to come in response to areas of tension. Administrators commonly react in response to a crisis and may often act only so far as to smooth things over.

But there have been a number of changes in Oxfordshire which do conform to a pattern of development: the blending of groups of handicapped children in special schools; the creation of units in ordinary schools; the merging of units into mainstream school activities; the transfer of teachers and groups of children from special into ordinary schools and hence an attempt towards the beginning of a dissolution of parallel systems of 'special' special and 'ordinary' special; the development of a conceptual framework for integration; the attempts to provide a unified service.

In 1970 the city and county of Oxfordshire had yet to be re-created, with a large area of North Berkshire, into the new administrative county authority under the 1974 local government reorganization. Two special schools in the town of Abingdon, in North Berkshire, Tesdale and Bennett House, were already experimenting with teaching mild and severely intellectually retarded children together (Jones, Burnham and Coles 1979). In the old county of Oxfordshire the 'unit' approach to meeting special needs in ordinary schools was being developed at Cooper School, Bicester (Garnett 1976; see also chapter 8, pp. 125–37). In 'units' the children tend to have the same disability and spend a very high proportion of their time separated from the rest of the school. But what was remarkable about the Cooper School development was the speed with which the 'unit' became a flexible 'resources' centre with children integrating into mainstream lessons.

Three purpose-built units for the mildly mentally retarded were opened and sited on the campus of comprehensive schools in 1976–77: it was to take a longer period for these to change their 'unit' image. Negotiations with the Department of Education and Science resulted in the building of a 'multi-handicap centre' at Carterton Comprehensive School and the monitored information obtained during the first two years of working provided the basis for a new policy initiative by the chief education officer which began in 1980.

A further step along the integration path took place at Banbury Comprehensive School when its physically seg-regated unit for the mildly mentally retarded, and its teaching staff of four, were integrated into the main system of the school. The children became part of normal tutor groups and were withdrawn for short periods to 'resource' rooms where a range of needs, not only for the slow learner, could be met. On this model of integration these 'special' children have become part of the normal spectrum of children with educational needs where the whole of the teaching staff gradually take a responsibility for meeting educational needs no matter where and how they are manifested.

Special school initiatives

Some of the heads of special schools in Oxfordshire, dissatisfied with the segregated role prescribed for them, attempted to find better ways of using their resources in more flexible styles of working. Some now place individual children out into ordinary schools with the special school teacher acting either in a consultancy role to mainstream teachers, or, where the staffing permits, physically assisting in ordinary schools: one special school for children with severe learning difficulties (an ESN(S) School) has placed two whole classes in a primary school and the children are taught by teachers who are part of the staff of the special school, and from September 1983 will place a third class in a neighbouring comprehensive; another special school has placed a group of physically handicapped teenagers out into a comprehensive school where the handicapped children are full-time members of ordinary classes and special school teachers work in the ordinary classes in a programme of team teaching.

Developing a conceptual framework

In the immediate post-Warnock period integration had focused on schemes and projects that aimed at reintegrating children with special needs into ordinary schools or at recreating the ethos of special schools within the ordinary school system (Hegarty and Pocklington 1981b, 1982). This 'limpet' approach, of attaching children to mainstream education in the hope that some of the waters of educational normality would wash over them, has been achieved (a) by placing children in units on the campus of ordinary schools or (b) by squeezing children with special needs into schools in the hope that somehow the ordinary school can 'stretch' its resources in order to cope with them (Jones 1983).

Instead of asking how certain children could be brought into mainstream education we have tried to look at ways to develop mainstream education so that fewer children would need to be put out into segregated provision. In the final analysis would there be any need to provide alternative segregated provision for any child with this approach? The answer is not known and will not be known until a school, a group of schools, or an LEA takes the initiative to find out.

We attempted to set out in a discussion document some of the principles that might inform the practices which would enable such a question to be answered (Jones and Jones 1980) and these included the following:

1 Special education should be seen as part of the continuum of extra provision in ordinary schools.
2 Children with special needs in ordinary schools should not be seen solely as the responsibility of 'special' teachers though teachers with specialized knowledge would be needed as part of the educational provision made available for such children. Normality is related to wholeness and the whole school staff are implicated in this concept.
3 Consideration should be given for all secondary schools to have departments of special needs with a head of department and special needs teachers. Special 'resource' centres may need to be set up in selected primary schools which would serve as a resource to a group of geographically close primaries or a group of primaries in scattered rural areas.
4 Some level of management would need to be set up that is less in size than a local education authority but larger than an individual school. A sector model is proposed where a local management group of heads could meet and plan local developments and where a sector would comprise of a secondary school and its associated primary schools.
5 To encourage local and sector identity special needs staff should be the responsibility of the heads of schools in which they have their working accommodation. The financing of such resources in ordinary schools would need to be a county commitment as extra resourcing to schools.

6   In such a model of management it would be expected that, as the Warnock Report proposed, there would no longer be a separation of function as between special needs departments and remedial departments and the practice of awarding special school allowances would be replaced by salary enhancement linked to qualifications and experience.

The Banbury initiative

The town of Banbury was chosen as the area for beginning to implement the proposals in the discussion document for a variety of reasons. It contained a mixed town community and included children from surrounding rural areas. It had schools ranging in school roll from 32 to 506 at the primary level and from 650 to 2,200 in the four secondary schools. Three of the comprehensives had special needs departments, two of which had departmental heads. In four of the primary schools there were special resource departments: one with a specialization towards children with language disorders; a second for children with partial hearing; a third for slow-learning children with associated home problems; and a fourth with an emphasis on children with behavioural and learning disabilities (see chapter 5 for a more detailed discussion.)

While the above factors were contributory to the locating of the special needs project in Banbury an overriding consideration was the favourable attitude of a number of heads towards integration.

A steering group committee was set up and chaired by the chief education officer. Its first problem was how to cope with the wide and diverse opinion and advice that was being fed into the project by those of differing views about the development of special education in Oxfordshire. Territorial issues surfaced rapidly and compromises were constantly being sought. Matters of principle tended to become translated into strategies for sustaining harmonious working arrangements between heads, advisers, administrators and support services.

A number of factors led the committee to propose the development of four sectors in the Banbury area each comprised of a comprehensive school and its feeder primaries. These included: the need for continuity of management from pre-school through the compulsory years to post–16 education as well as the active participation of parents in the area at all levels of decision-making in relation to their children's needs. In time a co-ordination between sectors was achieved through a 'Heads Executive' including the comprehensive head and a primary head from each of the four sectors and a county administrative officer, psychologist and special needs advisory teacher.

The issue of resources dominated early discussions. Members of the steering group were for the most part unaware of the extent of resources that existed in schools or of the principles that were applied that had resulted in imbalances as between schools. Resourcing had for the most part occurred out of individual schools' applications for additional staff and resources and was not balanced out against known needs across groups of schools. There was an immediate task, therefore, for heads to look at resources in the Banbury community, how these were being used, and what form of accountability there was for their effectiveness.

School-based support services

Lengthy discussions took place about the nature of appropriate administrative and support services. If it made no sense to segregate children with special needs, did it make any further sense to continue with 'segregated' administrative, advisory and support services?

The continued existence of such services, identified as they are with an administrator, advice and support, set apart from the ordinary services for education in general, and existing as a response to past policies of segregation philosophies and practices, tended only to perpetuate the 'institution' of segregation. What would be the alternative? To extend the work of ordinary assistant education officers so that special administration is encompassed within a framework of normal duties and to locate support services as far as possible within ordinary schools and as members of staff of ordinary schools:

this latter aspect would apply to teachers of special needs, education social workers, and psychologists.

The different sectors began to develop different styles of working. Banbury School sector opted to make all the support staff school-based: an extension of the 'normalization' principle beyond that to children. In the support services within the Banbury School sector there is a team of special needs teachers, some located and working only in the primary schools in the sector, some at secondary level, some in the college of further education, and some across the primary–secondary phase. There is also a school-based counsellor and educational psychologist (Jones *et al.* 1983). The project therefore has provided an opportunity for trying out a new style of working for the psychologist which creates new opportunities and its own difficulties. As a common member of the staff the psychologist has a new access to the inner life of the school which should enable a better understanding of factors that produce and alleviate school difficulties. There is the possibility of a closer working together with the school social worker, counsellor, special needs teachers, and main school staff on a day-to-day basis. The base in primary and secondary schools facilitates a relationship with families.Problems do arise, however, simply from the increased visibility of the psychologist's work. Erroneous expectations of a psychologist's knowledge and skills can be set up and these have to be dispelled. There is an immediately apparent overlap in the roles of all the support staff. There is a different form of accountability involved in fitting the work into the rhythms of the school day.

The problems of incrementalism

Once innovations become more generally applicable they begin to compete with existing management structures. Although a gradualist policy may facilitate the change process initially, there comes a time when critical decisions have to be made which set new patterns of working. In the meantime there is 'parallelism' in management. As an illustration of the problems that may arise consider a child with severe learning difficulties who was educated in one of the Banbury primary schools with the additional facilities of a special resources centre. When the child transferred to secondary school he found it difficult to move around from lesson to lesson. Additional welfare help was requested. At the same time there existed in a local special school seven teachers and an equal number of auxiliary helpers all of whom had knowledge and expertise in the educational management of children who are intellectually handicapped. Taken as a community, therefore, Banbury was well resourced to meet this area of special needs but the resources were not accessible to the ordinary school. Had there been resource rooms on the site of both selected secondary and primary schools staffed by teachers currently encapsulated in the special school, not only could the individual child described above have continued to receive a 'normal' education, but so could all the other intellectually handicapped children who were still in segregated provision.

In initiating an integration programme the LEA administrators soon discover that the resources that build up in mainstream schools are not compensated for by a readjustment in the segregated sector of special education. Two competing pools of resources are brought into existence. The ordinary schools cannot complete their programme of special development until such time as there is a freeing of resources currently frozen in special schools. The judgement is not necessarily whether to pursue a policy of running down segregated provision but in deciding whether mainstream resources are sufficiently developed so that the segregated net can be taken away to enable new roles for special schools to emerge.

Parallelism in management is likely to continue as long as scarce resources continue to be channelled into 'segregated' provision to meet the needs of a minute proportion of the school-age population; while the resource now being sought is from ordinary teachers in mainstream education. Parallelism comes in many forms and guises. It affects such minor details as who draws up the advertisements for new special needs staff, who shortlists, who is on the interview panels, and where the authority for the final choice of candidate is posited. Of more major importance it poses the question of who is accountable at advisory level for the new teachers in the sectors who will be specialized in areas of learning difficulty: the county primary adviser who has responsibility for the peripatetic remedial services or the special needs adviser under whose auspices the new staff are appointed according to one interpretation of the Warnock recommendation that 'remedial' should not be separated from 'special'?

In-service training tends to be an advisory function with meetings taking place away from ordinary schools in such places as teachers' centres. Teachers for such courses are drawn from a wide area of schools. In-service for integration involves all members of a given school and on topics that have arisen *within* the dialogue in ordinary schools: the traditional form of in-service planning and courses does not give way easily to the school-based format where ordinary heads take a priority role in deciding what courses are to be set up.

A particularly difficult area, where special needs become part of mainstream education, relates to the qualifications and experience of staff recruited. As the teaching profession, at secondary level, becomes a graduate profession, then those specializing in special needs, if only to achieve professional credibility, need also to have graduate status plus specialized knowledge. It is still common practice in the segregated area of special education to appoint non-graduates to advisory posts, as heads, as staff in special schools, and there grows a gap between those working in ordinary schools on special needs and those who are part of the support services who work on a peripatetic basis.

The change in practice from a 'unit' model of management to a 'resources approach' came slowly as individual heads and their staff, as at Cooper School, began to change their way of working. In some schools constraints are placed on this development either because of the way the curriculum timetable in the main school is constructed or because 'unit' styles of working lend themselves more easily to control and direction from outside the school, i.e. by LEA supervision, and such 'units' are organized much along the same lines as special schools from the point of view of LEA advisory and administrative practice. The basic studies department described by Hegarty and Pocklington, (1982, chapter 1) illustrates this well. But the major shifts in concept implicit in these changes have yet to be followed by a re-evaluation of teaching styles, financing in ordinary schools, and career structuring in special needs, which are still based on the unit principle and which continue to cause tension between county prescription and ordinary school practice. For as long as parallel philosophies inform management structures, there will be a strong tendency to continue with unit provision.

Concluding remarks

The past decade has seen significant shifts in emphasis in special education. A combination of factors has brought this about: pressure from parent groups; a reappraisal of more effective ways of utilizing scarce resources; legislative initiatives; a knowledge of practices in other countries; and curriculum developments. Examined in detail, however, and as illustrated in developments taking place in Oxfordshire, there is nowhere a systematic approach, at national or local authority level, to bring about change. Instead, there are individual school adjustments (a special class or teacher), or initiatives as between schools (sometimes between a special and ordinary school), or some pilot project related to part of the service of special education.

The debate, and indeed much of the research, focuses on what already appertains, and how this could be utilized to effect between services: its focal point is that of resources as related to teachers, skills, support services, equipment and buildings. To this extent issues about integration are not yet in the open, such as teachers' attitudes that determine integration outcomes in ordinary schools, and the channels for action still open to schools who are not prepared to make a local response, namely, the institutionalized practices within the concept of 'special education'. Nowhere does the concept of wholeness outlined above find expression in educational practice and the education provided still approximates to the disabilities of children. Special education orthodoxy still prescribes the way that children are identified, classified and grouped for teaching purposes (usually in units or special classes). The back-up for this is the array of assessors (usually psychologists, to be increased in number by some LEAs as a response to the 1981 Act without thought of what new roles might emerge were integration to be implemented and whether more of what has gone in the past will be required for the future); administrative procedures (to replace Special Education (SE) Form procedures with 'statement' procedures); and placement policy (by increased numbers of special advisers). All this focuses on specific need and classifiable disability.

The revolution in *ideas* as well as practice about integration has yet to gain momentum. The same number of children are still being segregated out of ordinary schools and the waiting lists remain; new special schools are being built and opened; there is still 'special' line management from the Department of Education and Science (and with HMI), through the university special needs departments and LEAs, down to heads and their governing bodies. As far as the 'institution' of special education is concerned, the innovations that have so far been achieved, mainly through individual initiatives rather than that of corporate policy-making, have constituted probably little more than a clearing away of the brushwood from around the Elizabethan castle.

5
A Comprehensive School for All

JOHN SAYER

The apparent tautology in the title of this chapter is deliberate and necessary in any treatment of integration. Most educators and most critics of secondary schooling now agree that comprehensive development has not yet gone far enough to justify its inelegant description. The term has emerged only within the post-war structure of secondary education, segregated not just from special but from primary, further, youth and adult education. The continuum with primary education, previously a fact for 80 per cent of the school population, was lost to all but special school pupils with the 1944 Education Act. Within secondary systems, comprehensive schools were derived largely from an amalgamation of pre-war secondary and upper elementary approaches, latterly described as secondary grammar and secondary modern schools. The amalgamation was achieved through the appeal of a 'grammar schools for all' still embodied in single-subject public examination objectives, once relevant to 25 per cent but now to 60 per cent of the school population. This spread of ability remains no more than might have been anticipated before the raising of the school-leaving age in 1973–74, and the rest of our young people have to fit into school organizations not adapted to their needs, or else become an appendage. Before comprehensive schooling gathered momentum, the technical elements of a nominally tripartite system were removed to the post-15 or post-16 population by a society which then began to complain that secondary schools were neglecting applications, manual and technical skills, and vocational preparation. The youth and adult education services have developed or rather contracted along their separate paths, sometimes dragging with them powers of community education, and only rarely has the community as a whole been seen as a client for comprehensive schools. Finally, independent education has remained enmeshed with purchased privilege, and it is rare to find a comprehensive school unaffected by social stratification. Only as one element, then, in this long list of segregated services does special education need to be added to the cause of integration.

This context may be helpful in determining the strategies required to integrate special and normal provision. It is evident that much is abnormal in the stage of normality we have reached and that there may not be much that is special in the adjustments required to meet needs previously served separately. Indeed, we now run the risk inside schools of replicating the single thrusts which have during the last century characterized the development of educational institutions, departments and professional structures. In the late nineteenth century, elementary schooling was ensured through local parish or borough school boards by the 1870 Forster Act. Another administrative structure emerged in 1888 with the creation of county and county borough authorities, which were subsequently enabled to establish technical schools, following the Samuelson Reports (Reports of the Royal Commission on Technical Instruction (1882, 1884) and secondary schools, following the Bryce Report (Report of the Royal Commission on Secondary Education (1895). Meanwhile, between 1899, when the Defective and Epileptic Children Act encouraged local authorities to make provision for special instruction, and 1944, when local authorities were required to ascertain the need for and to provide special educaitonal *treatment* 'in special schools or elsewhere', yet another branch of the local authority and of the teaching profession elaborated their own operations. The result of these separate stages of development is now an education service which exists only as a concept; a profession with distinctive career patterns and outlooks; local institutions which derive from each separate move; and, in a contracting service, jealous guardianship of boundaries. So when attempts are made to re-draw these boundaries according to criteria other than historical accident, they are often limited to an amalgamation of external structures, leaving much of the original separation within the internal organization, as well as the differences between the attitudes of teachers, the programmes and the pupils. Comprehensive schools reflect different stages of movement away from the tripartite division of pupils which the Spens Report (Board of Education 1938), the Norwood Report (Secondary Schools Examinations Council 1943) and the 1944 Education Act had so unsoundly established. Where they have been broadened to encompass local adult education, it has been despite the separate further education structures rather than because of them; the pattern of school-based youth tutor schemes demonstrates the same struggle against divided local and professional systems. Separate access to adult education wings, youth wings with separate management structures have many of the organizational characteristics of special education units attached to ordinary schools.

Within the notion of integration, there is a fundamental choice: whether to revise and extend what is seen as the current stage of normality or mainstreaming, in order to privide for all needs, be they termed special, vocational, lifelong or whatever, or to retain separate traditions cheek-by-jowl but in distinctive departments with their own power bases, leaving them to resolve or harden their differences in an externally unified structure, which enables them to coexist and society to believe that they are now in some way together.

Usually, it is the second of these that passes for integration and which is most readily acceptable to those whose experience has been in separate systems. Most of the case studies described in recent literature are of this kind: they are examples of integration in name alone, or of preserving separate traditions within the same structure, with minimal adjustments and benefits of shared resource, now commonly known as 'economies' (see Hegarty and Pocklington 1982). The alternative approach is daunting and goes beyond the immediate issue of integrating special education; indeed, it could and should lead to a revolution more far reaching than the movement I have described as comprehensive. What would it look like if all organized education in a local community were founded on the principle of reaching the whole of that community and resourced to meet all local needs? And how would provision for special educational needs then relate to the combined community service?

In a brief chapter, just a few shifts in practice may serve to illustrate what is desirable for the whole of a comprehensive community school as well as being necessary for the particular element of integration examined in this volume. Groupings, criteria for staffing, assessment and the management of resources are all central concerns for institutions as a whole; and they all radically affect the school's ability to meet special needs.

Schools are having to find their own solutions to each of these four problems, just as they are having to work out by experience how best to make themselves accessible to children with special needs. The excitement comes when a school realizes that all these separate strands belong together, conceptually and in practice. Banbury is no exception, and has now reached the point at which a new look at the whole framework for meeting children's needs has to be taken. I will illustrate two by describing some of the developments in the school away from a separate department for children with special needs.

Meeting special needs at Banbury School

The nationally funded research on groupings at Banbury (Newbold 1977; Postlethwaite and Denton 1978) threw up as its most usable finding one that is not recorded elsewhere in the existing literature: by 1975 it was evident that about three times as many children with a Verbal Reasoning Quotient of 70– were coming through primary schools undetected into the ordinary Halls (houses) of the school, as were being moved into the school's separate and remote department for the 'moderately subnormal, following official ascertainment. Having for other reasons become dissatisfied with the separation of the unit, its pupils and its teachers, we brought this special department together with the remedial department working in the mainstream, and after a year or two's phasing, all pupils became part of the ordinary tutorial groups and, therefore, for most of their time part of the ordinary teaching groups in the halls and upper school. This was not without its difficulties: some modification of fourth- and fifth-year options was found necessary (not just for the pupils transferred) and there was a heightened awareness that something much more radical was needed for the entire curriculum for all senior pupils. Nobody doubts, however, that the transfer was a good and necessary move.

Previously separate remedial provision for children with difficulties in literacy and numeracy, for children with physical impairments, for children with specific learning difficulties, for children with emotional and social problems, for English as a foreign language, could now be looked at as a whole; the new special needs department was no longer confined to a programme for dull children, but became a resource for all aspects of the school's work, a servicing department. This required of all teachers an ability to use a new resource and this is still being worked out, gradually and painfully.

The previously separate ESN(M) department had been for children from the age of 10, and this had to be altered. Banbury has always had an acute awareness of the problems of transfer from primary to secondary school. Although attempts in the mid-1970s to programme exchanges of primary and secondary teachers across the transfer age had been thwarted by cuts and a wave of 'siege economy' mentality, regular liaison meetings and a careful transfer system had been maintained for the mainstream, even though moves to the special department had been managed largely through support services with little connection with the school; the 'outer space' agencies. The senior assistant in the new special needs department now took on the task of primary school liaison for all pupils

Deep dissatisfaction with the level of resourcing and with criteria for special provision was responded to by the chief education officer who chaired for a year an area working party, with input from the different school 'sectors' (each comprehensive school and its partner primary schools). This helped to expose the different perceptions and levels of support available in different sectors. The sector group was accepted as a management unit for meeting special needs, and in the Banbury School sector it was possible to secure the appointment of a support teacher across the 10–14 age range for children with emotional or behavioural problems, and, through the bold initiative of the principal county psychologist, a sector educational psychologist. The former school principal's house was made over as a resource centre for these two, as well as for the existing school counsellor and the professional tutor. It also served as a convenient case conference venue but not as a unit for pupils. On behalf of all four comprehensive schools in the area there was a further appointment of a support teacher for the 14–17 age group, to work with the social services intermediate treatment worker and to contribute to the co-operation across services which had much the same clientele.

The continuum of response across primary and secondary schooling and beyond is no longer an optional extra but is built into the job description of teachers and other professionals working together. The management cycle of awareness, identification of problems, assessment of needs, prescription of response, resourcing and providing response, is common to all. This will probably survive even the miserably retarding effect of 'statement' procedures which are to follow the 1981 Education Act (Department of Education and Science 1983).

In six years, we have moved from having a separate unit off-site and a single-purpose withdrawal department on-site, towards a multi-professional servicing resource to enable all teachers to teach all pupils, and all pupils to share in an appropriate programme. But none of this can be understood without the context of the school as a whole, and the parallel developments that it shares with many others. The effects of groupings, assessment, staffing policies and resource management will amply illustrate the point.

Groupings

Teaching is conducted with a group of pupils, in primary and secondary schools usually a very large group; but children learn individually, the group experience being a stimulus, a hindrance or of no importance to individual learning. More because of a century's legislation than because of educational criteria, school systems are built around the assumption of a teacher working with a large group, all other activities being deviant to that organization. It is also assumed that children are best taught in isolation from adults, or that they should be taught with their immediate contemporaries whatever the level, skills or nature of study; it is an assumption that disappears after the 5–16 age span of compulsory schooling; education according to the date of birth. From these two assumptions spring many of the difficulties both in meeting the new and different demands upon education, and in continuing to meet many of the expectations that have long existed as part of the voluntary initiatives of schools rather than the formal legislative framework of provision. Musical instrument lessons, work experience, careers interviews, personal and curricular counselling, medical inspection, field studies, school journeys, individual or small group remedial work, although recognized as essential, become viewed as disruptive, or as an extraction as undesirable as the dental variety, it being assumed that children, like teeth, belong in rows.

Which rows? It is more usual for a school to have a detailed scheme of work to be covered in each subject than to have a detailed policy on groupings. School is itself a decision on groupings: the ordinary school is a form of special education by withdrawal from the basic educative unit of the family and its immediate environment, and is set up to meet specific needs which cannot always be met in that normal setting. The groupings set up in a school may reflect continuity or a deliberate attempt to break it for social or academic reasons. Decisions are likely to be founded on half-truths, or on a balance of gain and loss given the large-group basis of the whole enterprise. Since secondary education is largely subject-based, however appropriately, the pressure is likely to be for immediate gains in subject learning, and therefore for grouping by levels of attainment; and since schools are organized in year groups as a result of legislation, this will result in chronological streaming or setting by subject. The first will have a general effect of depressing those who for any reason at any stage are slower performers; the second, a refinement, will have the effect of breaking up the identity of form groups.

Before rejecting what usually happens, let us remember that teachers must be enabled to teach, and that any decision is about gains as well as losses. There are learning activities in which it is helpful for those who have reached a similar level to work on together; one school decided on mixed ability for all activities except games, which were streamed, and whilst this is unusual in school contexts, it would be seen as common sense by the local and national league systems of association football which occupy the minds of very many in the community, and for which school games might be seen by some as a preparation. The objection to streaming or setting is that it is viewed as the starting point, on behalf of subject teaching, leaving the overall needs of each pupil and the overall social aims of the school and community to be reflected in an artificial and cosmetic overlay of pastoral care.

Groups which are socially and academically balanced, or mixed, may have to be contrived for housing policies are not founded on educational principles, and the community served by a comprehensive school is probably divided deeply by public and private sectors, by declining inner and more recent suburban or commuter village areas. Each of these will be served by its own primary school; so each primary school may reflect a privileged or deprived immediate environment. Should a comprehensive school go for continuity and perpetuate the social divisions of local housing, or should this be sacrificed in order to bring together a future society? The balance of gain or loss has to be determined in each local situation, but groupings in schools will have a social effect, whether or not it is consciously planned, and whatever the balance of gain, there will have to be compensation for losses too.

How does this relate to provision for special needs? Special schools and special unit bases for slow learners are a form of segregation by streaming. If the social and tutorial base of a school favours a balance of abilities, and perhaps even better a balance of ages too, there is nothing special about moving out to individual programmes; in terms of institutional management, extraction for an instrumental lesson, for a counselling session, for an individual subject option, or for remedial attention, are all of a similar nature. But if such a group is resourced for individually paced learning or for small-group work, it becomes legitimate to ask whether it is best to withdraw a pupil for small-group work elsewhere, or to provide the appropriate resource in the ordinary class context. And that resource may be help from other pupils; the resource may be team teaching, with another teacher or ancillary working in the same group; it may be individual programme resource material, or elements of all these. The group at Banbury is now being organized and resourced to involve each pupil appropriately.

The difficulty is not just one of preparing ourselves as teachers to use resources in this way; so far, no serious work has been undertaken to identify the criteria for resourcing mainstream teaching groups to enable them to provide for varieties of special need. Research is urgently required into the nature of preventive support and preventive resource, so that current strategies of crisis management or case conferences more appropriate to a coroner's court can be reduced to a minimum.

In a preliminary exercise, I have explored teachers' perceptions of the resource needed to meet the needs of a sample of pupils, and have set down what teachers consider to be the best and most cost-effective blend of group size, ancillary provision, support teaching and specific resource (Sayer 1982). Already this has shown that no existing staffing or resourcing formulae, whether imported from special education or not, are applicable. Any such formula must take into account the skills of teachers and other professionals available; appropriate teaching materials and equipment; ancillary help in the background or in the group; time to consult before and after teaching; the size of teaching groups; additional time with particular pupils; the ability of the group as a whole to cope with the needs of individual pupils. There must be some attempt to provide *equivalent* resources to different areas according to local needs. What is now required is a multi-professional approach to prescription, resourcing and assessment within a local context.

Criteria for staffing

The withdrawal of a teacher, for whatever good reason, is as disruptive as individual learning activities for pupils if the single teacher with a large class group is a rigid organising principle of the school. One school may have as many as 10,000 'staff substitutions' in a year, and the time required to organize these is as great as that required to organize the original timetable from which teachers are withdrawn. The extraction of a teacher may be to respond to an individual pupil or family crisis, to attend an in-service course, to conduct a school visit, to make contact with other local services, to conduct a specialized examination. Because of the growing variety of demands and expectations on schools, these activities are increasing rapidly, and are at odds with the starting management assumptions according to which a teacher is timetabled with a large class determined by a pupil–teacher ratio.

Whereas it is a minor irritant to have a visiting professional extract pupils individually – an instrumental teacher, foreign language assistant, educational psychologist, school doctor or therapist, researcher, or even a holiday-bound parent – the problem is magnified if it is organized from within the school, without planned resourcing. If a school itself determines that there shall be individual contact, counselling, remediation, family liaison, school camps or visits, daytime concerts, there is only one way in which it can be achieved: by giving less staff time to ordinary class teaching and putting more of the same time into individual, small-group or one-off activities. This is superficially attractive: we cannot give adequate individual attention within the large group, so we have colleagues available to extract pupils, apparently thereby reducing the size of the group. In fact, of course, by planning to have teachers available for individual attention without having had this budgeted and provided for, we have fewer teachers to deploy across the large groups, and therefore make the starting size of classes larger, so creating the very problems which call for individual attention. We are caught in a spiral of mis-management.

Partly because of this wrong basis of staffing (see also Sayer 1980, and chapter 9), schools are likely to be places of even greater stress and frustration in a time of falling rolls. As government promptings encourage a drab minimum curriculum as the basis for protected group staffing, those extension activities which have by now become part of the personal expectation for pupils will be the first to be undermined. And it is because of this failure in management that the challenge of integration may be feared as an added burden in the absence of a radical change in approaches to staffing. Something has to be done anyway, and it may be that issues of integration will serve to remind us that there are still no agreed criteria for the staffing of schools, at least south of the border (SED 1973).

This is doubly true of ancillary or auxiliary staffing, and of specialized education services. If local education committees have little idea what teachers do, they have even less inkling of the contribution that can be made by educational psychologists, counsellors, education social workers, youth tutors, careers officers, or child guidance services. Teachers' associations do little to enlighten them locally, because by and large teachers do not have much idea either. As for ancillaries and auxiliaries, there have never been carefully formulated criteria for the support they give to teachers in ordinary schools or for their working relationship to teaching colleagues. If it is true that there need to be well-considered policies for their provision, to meet special needs, this is only one part of a problem already there in comprehensive schools, and one which has an even greater bearing on the development of community schooling. The education of children with special needs brings with it overt acceptance of multi-professional and inter-professional support. It may not yet be accepted throughout an education service that, as Richard Titmuss claimed:

> the blurring of the hitherto sharp lines of demarcation between home care and institutional care, between physical disability and mental disability, between educationally backward children and so-called 'delinquent' children, and between health needs and welfare needs, is all part of a general movement towards more effective services for the public and towards a more holistic interpretation and definition of the principles of

primary, secondary and tertiary prevention. On a broader plane, society is moving towards a symbiosis which sees the physician, the teacher and the social worker as social services professionals with common objectives. (Titmuss 1968, p. 63)

If, however, we can achieve this in the mainstream for children with special educational needs, we may be moving the whole of our service in that direction.

Assessment

Skills of assessment have remained underdeveloped and underused inside the schools. There has been too great a dependency on external modes of examining pupils' achievements in particular subjects, and much of the school curriculum and methodology has been geared to performance at 16. Assessment of need, potential and progress, from which educational programmes could be derived, has been largely haphazard in mainstream schools, and has not been included in the staff time allocated to schools.

External examinations at 16 have become irrelevant both to the needs of pupils and to the requirements of future employers or educational establishments: any employment available at 16 is secured before results are published and probably even before examinations are sat; and continuing education is most appropriately agreed as a result of counselling and professional judgement well before the examination season. For the large proportion of pupils for whom such examinations were not designed, they are a tool of social rejection, cancelling much that a comprehensive school has sought to achieve for its society. This has been a particularly acute problem since the raising of the school-leaving age, and will not be touched by any common system of examining which may emerge from current proposals and wranglings.

Two more recent developments are likely to eclipse this whole sphere of sterile procedures. The first is the consensus forced on society by rapidly rising unemployment, but sought for more positive reasons by most educators long before, that all young people to the age of 18 should be seen to be engaged in education and training, whether based in educational establishments or places of employment. The second is the growing acceptance that a profile of needs, programmes, experience and competencies should be built up for each young person throughout education and across into the training offered in employment.

The development of profiling is largely incompatible with the dominance of public examining. It is much more likely to be compatible with a general approach to resourcing needs and with a developmental view of the education process. It is also much more likely to bring skills of assessment in from the cold, and have them seen as part of the teaching and learning transaction. This has implications for the make-up of a comprehensive school staff, for professional skills practised across institutional divides, and for inter-professional transactions.

Educators with trained skills in assessment have been isolated from the mainstream service, largely by the management process through which their services are sought. Educational psychologists in particular have not been perceived to belong anywhere. The writer spent 18 years in secondary education before knowingly meeting one. Certainly, at secondary level, they have not been consulted until a problem is apparent, and usually when it has resisted all internal solutions. They are not in a position to understand the whole complex structure of a comprehensive school, and therefore are not in the best position to advise on the future handling of the problem, except by referral to the outer space with which they have been most associated, special schooling. They cannot readily become part of the support which will prevent problems reaching crisis stage. Like public examinations, they are left to the end. Their skills have not been made available through transmission to teachers. It is no small wonder that many educational psychologists are wishing to extend beyond and away from diagnostic testing and assessment, towards intervention, training and therapy.

These skills of diagnostic testing and assessment are, however, sadly lacking in schools, and they are necessary for effective teaching as they are in any management cycle.

Perhaps it may be seen to be appropriate in a community school to have educational psychologists as part of the management resource and as involved in policy-making as teachers. They will then become part of the inner core of resource and guidance available to all teachers, parents and pupils, thus improving a school's response to needs. Again, the effect will be to make it unnecessary to refer pupils for placement to a separate special service.

Resource management

For positive reasons and for negative ones, the second half of the 1980s will be characterized by a more local approach to education services. The negative reasons have to do with falling rolls, political priorities which place education low on the list and a declining economy, all of which will lead to an attempt by central and local authorities to provide guidelines where they cannot provide resources, and to devolve upon the local community and its existing institutions the task of making ends meet as best they can. The positive reasons are that this would be a healthy approach in any circumstances. A really local service, by which we understand one which is within reach and known to the whole community, will embrace not just all the educational institutions but probably at least the social services as well in some federated form, balancing a sense of identity in each part with a flexible total resource available to all. The concept of a federal education centre is likely to emerge as more important than all the side issues, patch-preservation and power-seeking which go into decisions on school closures and amalgamations, post-16 arrrangements, or staking out the claim to special education. What is coming can already be seen in Coventry (Coventry Education Department 1981) and in Bradford with its 'commonwealth' of schools and colleges, and in many smaller localities. Federal schools or federations of schools and colleges will have the task of finding a balance between total resource for flexible response to needs, and the identity of smaller personal communities in which pupils, parents and teachers feel they belong and for which they feel responsible. But there are plenty of models in and outside education.

Prompted by whatever contingency, federal systems are conducive to more open and more flexible responses to new situations and needs. They can work, however, only with a shared awareness of the wider education service and its place in the life of the local community. These are rapid and radical developments in the mainstream of educational provision. They are also necessary if we are to bring together resources which were previously organized separately as ordinary, special or associated services. They may well be the way towards making better sense both of education and social services, in their shared responsibility to meet special needs in the community.

Given a sense of common commitment to a particular community, and some form of federation through which resources can be allocated according to priority needs, initiatives from voluntary sources can be brought together much more effectively with planned public provision. This is not to suggest that inadequate public provision should be supplemented from private incomes. Rather, it is a reminder that parents, centres of employment, and the local community as a whole have an educative role without which schools cannot contribute effectively; and that the energies and initiatives of teachers and others account for much that is memorable in school experience. The local community, through its stake in education, has some chance of becoming a community in more than the geographical sense. The community school can become a place in which all are able to participate in meeting the challenge of survival for an education service, and determining areas of positive discrimination.

The wider the range of needs being served by a comprehensive school, the more likely it becomes that traditional school opening hours give way to a total use of the physical resource; this in turn requires a planning of the totality of educational activities, more flexible use of professional time, and a different kind of management and finance structure. It is no longer appropriate for each kind of activity to be linked with a separate section of a local government office; a new kind of organism is being created, generating its own activities, and requiring pointers and encouragement from local and central government rather than specific and detailed provision. The school and its community may become increasingly responsible for determining their own funding priorities.

We have reached the stage of realizing that the continuum of response advocated by the Warnock Committee is incompatible with its simultaneous perpetuation of separate services and heightened specialism. Through the issues raised by meeting special education needs, we have our best opportunity to establish that all education is about responses to all individual needs. The revolution in concept and evolution in awareness have not been caused by the integration of children with special needs, but in some circumstances may certainly have been triggered off by attention to this particular issue. The 1943 White Paper suggested that: 'Education in the future must be a process of gradually widening horizons, from the family to the local community, from the community to the nation, and from the nation to the world' (Board of Education 1943). In effect, what we are trying to do is to extend the meaning of the comprehensive school so that it becomes truly comprehensive in spirit and has a basic resource to enable it to make an increasingly comprehensive response to the needs of all children and families in the locality.

6
Who is Responsible for Children with Special Needs?

TONY DESSENT

I am a local authority educational psychologist who is interested in the development of integrated facilities for children with special needs. I believe that despite the many pushes towards 'integration' brought about by Warnock and recent legislation, the creation of more integrated facilities, which can properly meet children's individual needs, will be difficult to achieve. There are a number of problems to solve and resolve. My belief is that the major issues relate to the question of *responsibility*: administrative, professional and personal responsibility for handicapped and difficult-to-teach children. To begin with, we need to explore the ways in which responsibility for children with special needs is assigned and then ask the question: 'How, in an integrated system, should responsibility for special needs be allocated?' In order to understand what is going on at the moment it is helpful to view special education as primarily a system of *responsibility assignment* in local education authorities. Whatever else special education involves it is first and foremost an administrative and organizational system whereby one group of professionals are invested with responsibility for handicapped and 'difficult-to-teach' children. At the same time other groups are absolved from such responsibility. Special education has come to be described and justified (particularly to parents of children about to enter the system) in terms of its small teaching groups, special curricula, expertise and methods, but its historical roots lie in the need to remove responsibility for teaching children with special needs from class teachers in normal schools. Special education still provides this important psychological function for mainstream staff. At the most obvious level we can identify the personnel (teachers, psychologists, doctors and advisers) in whom responsibility comes to be invested, but it is also worthwhile exploring the transference of both professional and *personal* responsibility which occurs with children who are identified as having special needs. One interesting aspect of this process is the fact that the need for removal or transference of responsibility is greater with some groups of 'special' children than with others and there is often *an inverse relationship to the severity of the child's handicap*. Most of the children referred to educational psycologists for possible transfer to special schools have learning or behaviour difficulties and no apparent physical disability. Frequently, in the same classroom is a child with sensory or physical handicaps and often greater learning or behavioural difficulties who is regarded as appropriately placed within a normal classroom. Schools find it more difficult to assume continued responsibility for children without visible handicaps presumably because they pose a threat in some direct way to the teachers' feelings of professional competence.

Most psychologists have experienced the relative ease with which hearing impaired, visually handicapped and physically handicapped children can be integrated into normal schools in comparison with other groups. Most reports of successful integration attempts relate to children with sensory or physical handicaps. Special needs are often thought to be synonymous with 'hard' physical handicaps, and, not surprisingly, when the Warnock Report findings were published by the *Times Educational Supplement* its front page carried a large photograph of children with physical disabilities with wheelchairs, elbow crutches and specialized equipment in abundance. The majority of the children with whom the report was concerned, however, have no such visible handicaps. Teachers will often comment that integration is possible with children who are of 'normal ability' and can pursue normal curricula. However, my own experiences in integrating a small number of mentally handicapped children into ordinary schools indicate that the 'ability' factor is not the key issue. What is of greater importance is the fact that teachers can *see* the reason for the child's difficulties and both parents and

teachers can more readily agree upon the nature of the
problem. When handicaps are visible teachers can more readily
assume responsibility for the child's learning, education and
problems. Resources, too, can be made more readily available
at an administrative level for 'countable' numbers of children
with visible handicaps (for example, additional ancillary staff
and specialized equipment). The implications for integration
are clear and are already being realized. One could envisage the
situation where large numbers of children with 'hard'
handicaps are integrated into ordinary schools whereas the
vast majority of special needs children with moderate learning
and social difficulties remain in segregated provision.

Responsibility is also more readily accepted for another
group of children: those whose parents are regarded as having
an 'appropriate and realistic understanding of their children's
needs'. The identification of parents as 'difficult' and 'unco-
operative' is frequently a contributing factor in the referral of a
child for segregated special education and a large part of the
responsibility that special schools assume for children with
special needs relates to their dealings with the children's
parents. The social definition and causation of special
educational needs is clear in this context. Many families have
multiple needs and can be demanding of time and attention of
staff in ordinary schools. The social and family difficulties
which parents will frequently discuss with class teachers and
headteachers will often alarm and frighten the teaching staff
concerned. This may precipitate a move towards referral and
the sharing of responsibility for the problems with outside
agencies.

The strong need on the part of some teachers to have a
child's difficulties labelled and categorized is similarly related
to personal and professional feelings of responsibility. On one
occasion I talked to a group of primary headteachers about the
demise of assessment procedures which lead to the
categorization and labelling of children's difficulties and
suggested to them an approach more closely related to their
future educational needs. One experienced headteacher
commented that while she agreed with this 'new' approach she
was still aware that her class teachers 'breathed a sigh of relief'
when an educational psychologist came into the school and

declared a child to be dyslexic, aphasic, brain-injured and so on, because at least it meant that the child's failure was no fault of theirs.

A central feature of the educational psychologist's role in special education is the job of *defining responsibility* for special educational needs. His or her local authority employers, and indeed schools themselves, may care little for the detail of his assessment and diagnostic procedures so long as this central administrative role in special education is performed. The vast majority of referrals to an educational psychologist can be regarded as questions along the lines of: 'Is this child our responsibility or somebody else's?' (special school, remedial services, child guidance). Psychologists in most areas could easily list 'good' and 'bad' schools in terms of the schools' ability to cater for children with special needs. 'Good' schools are identified by the fact that the head and class teachers within the school assume personal and professional responsibility for teaching *all* children in their area rather than by the possession of any particular technical expertise, teaching approaches or methods of organization. Such schools require dramatically less involvement from psychologists as definers of special needs. School psychological services and related services (child guidance, child psychiatry) have a built-in survival mechanism by virtue of their role as definers and sharers of responsibility for special needs children. One quickly becomes aware as a psychologist that by simply visiting a school and talking to or listening to the teacher of a referred child you are often regarded as providing a useful service because in so doing the responsibility for the child is shared with you and often imperceptibly transferred to you!

I have touched briefly on some aspects of ordinary schools and support services as they relate to this issue of responsibility for children with special needs. What of special schools themselves? Clearly special schools represent a neat and tidy administrative solution to the problem of assigning responsibility for children with special needs. Indeed the great strength of segregated special schools lies in their administrative and financial simplicity. This rather than philosophical, educational or egalitarian principles is likely to be an important factor in determining the rate at which more integrated provision occurs.

As a local authority educational psychologist and a lukewarm behaviourist, I am aware that my behaviour of assigning children to special schools is continually rewarded. The problems of children who were apparently failing, troublesome, unhappy, truanting, suspended and so on in ordinary schools seem to disappear and melt away upon entry into special education. The reasons, I would maintain, have less to do with small group teaching and the expertise of staff than the fact that the children have become the responsibility of those specifically employed to carry it for 'difficult-to-teach' children. What is clear is that from the point of view of an educational psychologist the children could be, and often are, forgotten about. In contrast the often *ad hoc* attempts at integrated education that I have been involved in can lead to punishing consequences for myself as a psychologist. Psychologists in these situations often find themselves being held responsible for every facet of the child's educational development. There is no special school headteacher or similar figure monitoring and taking decisions regarding the child's class placement, educational programme, behavioural difficulties, parental concerns, anxieties and so on. Small-scale and *ad hoc* attempts at integration of this kind quickly make one aware of the administrative advantages of special schools which involve a complex investment of responsibility among its personnel for special needs children and often (just as importantly) their families.

I do think that special schools have some educational and resource advantages because of their size and separateness. I was recently discussing with a senior teacher in a special school the possibility of special school staff working with special needs children in normal schools. His response was that few staff in special schools would *choose* to work in ordinary schools. His point was that special school teachers had opted into special education to work in conjunction with like-minded staff (those, as he put it, 'interested in children rather than subjects'), and that only in a special school could the development of resources as well as mutual support and informal training for staff occur. The point is an important one. There are a number of other more mundane but nonetheless important issues. For example the ability of large special schools to raise funds to purchase the school minibus, video and computer equipment and so on. How many units attached to normal schools can boast their own minibus? Integration is not simply a matter of replacing special schools by building unit provision or relocating special school staff within the mainstream. It also involves us in designing facilities which can incorporate the administrative and educational advantages of special schools into the mainstream. In my view this is the single most important research question yet to be answered in the field of special education.

The tendency to segregate responsibility for children with special needs is both cause and effect of a segregated special education system. The tendency is maintained by the fact that advisory, administrative and financial segregation also occurs in most local education authorities. Special education has its own budget, its own administrative and advisory officers. The consequences can be critical for any movement towards a more integrated system. Having recently been involved in the relocation of part of a special school into a mainstream school, I have abruptly been made aware of the administrative complexities and pitfalls, for example differing capitation allowances for children in special schools from those in ordinary schools, special schools' allowances paid to teachers; special allowances paid to ancillary staff in special schools but perhaps not in ordinary schools; establishing lines of responsibility for special education staff.

In addition, obtaining the necessary resources and finance for integrated facilities can be problematic when the administration of finance for special education makes little or no allowance for the fact that special education can occur in ordinary as well as special schools. I am thinking here particularly about the provision of ancillary helpers and specialist equipment for physical handicapped children attending normal schools. I have heard of situations where £10 or £20 for a specialist piece of equipment for a child attending an ordinary school has created untold administrative difficulties, whereas £5,000 for a residential special school can be found with relative ease. The problem is simply one of the allocation of money by administrators to various arbitrary headings.

Implications for an integrated system

I have argued that special education has been viewed as primarily a process whereby both professional and personal responsibility for children with special needs is transferred from one group (teachers, advisers and administrators involved in mainstream education) to another group (the 'special educators'). But for an integrated system we have to consider how special education can be organized so that a genuine sharing of responsibility between these two groups can occur. Integration can be looked at purely in terms of the transfer from special to ordinary schools of children with special needs, special school staff and resources. More important for its ultimate success will be this transfer of personal and professional responsibility for the children. Changing the location of special education from special to ordinary schools, while certainly aiding such a transfer, will not guarantee it, as the experience of many of those working in isolated special units in ordinary schools will attest. What implications, then, can be drawn from this perspective for the development of an integrated system? My own feeling is that clear and unequivocal legislation and/or local authority policy is an important, but now probably unattainable, first step in the process of transferring responsibility for children with special needs. Beyond this there appear to be a number of important changes to the way in which services are administered, which, if made, would aid the development of integrated facilities.

1 *Integration of the categories.* The creation of integrated facilities for the generic group 'children with special needs' rather than the piecemeal 'unitization' of separate categories of handicap is one possible solution to the problem that responsibility for some groups/categories of handicapped children is more readily assumed than for others. We should look towards the development of 'special needs' departments/units rather than facilities catering for 'learning

difficulties', 'behavioural difficulties' and so on. How far can we go on this path? What about the 'hard' handicaps: visual impairment, hearing impairment, physical handicap? These latter groups both more easily attract resources and are more readily integrated within the mainstream. They tend to be isolated from other areas of special need whether within special or mainstream schools. But the reality is that many children with sensory and physical handicaps have multiple difficulties and their curriculum needs are not widely dissimilar from those of other groups of children with special needs. There will of course be a need for specialist teaching and equipment for some groups. Nevertheless, one of the great myths that has developed in the field of special education is that there are clear differences between the curriculum and teaching needs of the various groups of children with special needs. The way in which provision is made for the 2 per cent of children with significant and exceptional special needs will have a powerful influence on the way in which the needs of Warnock's 20 per cent are (or are not) met. It is difficult to imagine how a resource base for 'children with special needs' in a primary school could maintain a physically handicapped child with complex learning and perceptual difficulties and a visually impaired child with associated learning difficulties, on an integrated programme but be unable to cater for a physically 'normal' socially deprived child with learning difficulties. In developing generic facilities in mainstream schools specialist teachers and ancillary staff must have responsibility for children with more moderate (perhaps 'non-statemented' children) within the base school. Inclusion of these children will entail some complex arithmetic from administrators concerned with establishing staffing levels. Increasing the proximity of special provision to normal provision faces the problem squarely of *who are* the children with special needs which then leads to the question of *how many* children there are (for example, in a comprehensive school). The building of separate special school or unit provision has provided an easy answer to such questions and their administrative simplicity in large part accounts for the rapid development of separate special education facilities since 1944.

2   *Incorporating the strengths of special schools.* In planning

integrated facilities a major aim should be the creation of services that incorporate the administrative, professional and educational assets of special schools. Units, resource bases and other integrated provisions are frequently organized with unclear lines of authority and responsibility. There is rarely a figure with the same status and responsibility as that of a headteacher of a special school. Many integrated facilities 'leak'; children move from them to special schools partly because of organizational inadequacies. There are problems with regard to career structure for staff working with children with special needs in mainstream units. Where do able teachers go after reaching a scale 3 post? How can we ensure that the development of appropriate curricula and expertise occurs if special education staff are scattered thinly within mainstream schools. These are just some of the problems to be resolved and the questions to be answered if the very real advantages which special schools enjoy are to be transferred to a more integrated system. We need to think carefully about the number of special needs staff working within any one mainstream school, the development of resource centre bases for staff and the development of senior advisory/teaching posts in order to ensure co-ordination of the work of special needs staff. In short there is a need to construct an integrated system which is hierarchical for career purposes and supportive at the level of classroom teaching but which does not separate out special needs staff in terms of allegiances and responsibility from mainstream staff. Such a system has yet to be developed.

3 *Finance and resource 'integration'*. As long as the financing and resourcing of special education is carried out in isolation from the financing and resourcing of mainstream education, the potential for developing more integrated facilities will not be realized. Of particular importance is the fact that resources for special needs should be equally available and equally accessible to children in normal schools as in special schools and units. This does not stop simply at the level of obtaining specialized equipment and staff for small numbers of handicapped pupils, although this is important. It must ultimately go much further. The location of a 'special needs department' in a school would need to involve a rethinking of the school's existing staffing and resources in order to ensure

that the children could enjoy a range of experiences linked to normal classes. Appropriate increases in staff at all levels would probably need to occur: teachers, ancillaries, as well as secretarial and perhaps dinner supervisory staff! The flexibility required here is unlikely to occur while the administrative and advisory structures that underpin special education remain separate.

4   *'Sharing responsibility'*. How can this genuinely occur at all levels of the system? At the level of a mainstream school it seems clear that responsibility for special needs children cannot be totally in the hands of a headteacher. Heads are subject to too many powerful and competing pressures. The children concerned are a vulnerable group who may have little weight in the competition for resources when pitted against other needs such as the sixth form and examination successes. The dilemma is that genuine responsibility for special needs can occur in mainsteam education only when the broad aims of the system uphold the needs of individual children as of paramount importance rather than examination and occupational success. Until this occurs, special needs children will need to be protected by factors and agencies external to the school. The challenge for the future is the development of a carefully balanced sharing of responsibility between mainstream and special education staff which maximizes the children's access to and opportunities within normal schools.

7
Curriculum Principles for Integration

WILL SWANN

Introduction

In discussions about integration it is often asked: 'How do we preserve the special school curriculum for children when they are transferred to the mainstream?' The approach yields some positive results. It directs attention to the practicalities of dispersing materials and staff over a large number of schools, and to the need to preserve a measure of positive discrimination to ensure the availability of equipment, expertise and attention. But the question is also limited and defective, for it assumes that the curriculum of a special school ought to be applied in an ordinary school. The first response to the question: 'How do you preserve the curriculum?' should be: 'What parts should be preserved?' and then: 'How do you preserve them?'

In this chapter I shall argue that prevalent conceptions of the special curriculum impede integration. First, I shall discuss the common view of the curriculum as a set of teaching plans rather than the effect of schooling on children's experience and describe the way this separates issues of 'organization' from 'curriculum' and hence removes the integration debate from the agenda of curriculum development for children in special schools.

Secondly, I shall look at the extent to which specialized curricula actually exist in special schools and at the pressure to increase their specialization and hence reduce the access of children to the curriculum of ordinary schools. Thirdly, I shall explore the way the conception of the curriculum as teacher plans, and the tendency to specialization, are combined in the current emphasis given to the use of behavioural objectives as a basis for the special curriculum and examine some of the problems associated with this approach. Finally, I shall describe some principles for an integrated curriculum.

Conceptions of the curriculum

Approaches to curriculum development
The view of the curriculum as a set of teaching plans predominates in special education. A DES booklet *Educating Mentally Handicapped Children* described the curriculum, typically, as 'a school's plan for facilitating a child's growth and for developing selected skills, ideas, attitudes and values' (DES, 1975). Of course, this view is also widely adopted in mainstream education. If one sees the curriculum as a written plan, it follows that curriculum development is primarily a process of examining and elaborating plans. These may take the form of lists of aims and objectives, timetables, individualized programmes, checklists of achievements, and so on. By taking this view of the curriculum schools may be judged according to what the staff has written down about them rather than classroom practices. A common criticism of special schools is that they often have no written curriculum plan that they can hand out to enquiring visitors, inspectors and research workers (Brennan, 1979; Leeming *et al.* 1979). Conversely, a small number of special schools have published their own curriculum plan. Sometimes these are highly elaborate and complex, such as the work of Rectory Paddock School, Bromley. The existence of such a detailed plan itself is frequently a source of approbation.

   While it is important for teachers to plan in advance how they will spend time with a group of children, plans should not be the sole focus of curriculum study and development. They can only ever be very general guides to practice. There is always a gap between the intentions of a teacher and their realization in the classroom, both because the teacher's actions may have unforeseen consequences and because much of the activity in classrooms is unrelated to curriculum planning. The same plan can be put into practice by two teachers in two entirely different ways with two different outcomes, by virtue of the teachers' characteristics as people and their personal relationships with their pupils. If we want to understand the education of children we have to view their total experience in school. Simply elaborating a plan deals with only part of that experience.

Stenhouse (1975, p.3) summarized the distance between plan and practice as 'not unlike that between Haig's headquarters and the mud of Flanders'. He was one of a number of educationalists who, during the 1970s, argued that curriculum study should be concerned with the relationship between the teaching plan and empirical analyses of classroom practice: 'an adequate theory should be advancing our knowledge of the situation so that unanticipated results become susceptible of anticipation' (Stenhouse 1975, p.77). Curriculum development involved bringing practice in classrooms and teaching plans closer together through an evaluation of classroom practice by teachers. This model of curriculum development has had very little impact on special education. The idea that improving teaching should begin with understanding learning and teaching has played little part in writings on the special curriculum. Few people have argued that curriculum development should begin from a detailed and sympathetic understanding of classroom life, and how it is perceived by the participants. But without a critical understanding of day-to-day life in classrooms, it is impossible to understand the impact of curriculum innovations and thus to innovate more sensitively and more successfully. In a study of one day school for mentally handicapped children, the head of the school tried to co-ordinate the work of different teachers by introducing developmental checklists under a number of headings. He intended that teachers should select from these skills to teach, and to use the checklist as a basis for an annual review of children's progress. However, the implementation of this programme was complicated by the staff's approach to their own work. They found it very difficult to order their activity with the checklists. One teacher remarked:

> I feel sometimes as if we work from an academic point of view simply to get our minds straight. It's totally

unrealistic to pretend that you can just plough through this programme and move from Stage 1 to Stage 2 in a normal way because these children's reactions are so unpredictable. There's no way you can plan for the child's development, no theory to help you understand it. The only way to deal with it is by sheer spontaneity and instinct. (Flynn and Swann 1982, p.345)

If we define the curriculum to include the total experience of children in school, then Stenhouse's approach takes us only part of the way towards an analysis of that experience and we cannot develop a curriculum critique simply by an evaluation of classroom practice. There are many features of special school life, for example, that have a major impact on children, features that are beyond the control of individual teachers. These include the other children in the school, the school's resources, its location, its relationship with the parents and the wider community, perceptions of the school by the community and by mainstream schools. All these give rise to significant experiences that are unique to special schooling. In addition, it is also important to understand what experiences children are denied through their removal from ordinary schools. Many of these factors may be traditionally classified under the heading of 'organization', rather than 'curriculum'. But if curriculum development consists of attempts to understand and enhance the school lives of children, then such an artificial distinction must be untenable. In special education the dichotomy has the effect of excluding the integration debate from discussions of the curriculum.

The experience of special schooling: a hidden curriculum?
Features of school experience not overtly subject to teacher plans are sometimes called 'the hidden curriculum', though it should be recognized that educators hide themselves from aspects of children's experiences which are frequently obvious to children and their parents. Most obvious to many handicapped children is their removal from ordinary children and their being surrounded by other handicapped children. They are reminded thereby that a relatively minor part of them has already had a major impact on the quality of their lives.

What lessons do they learn simply by being continually in the company of other children with a similar disability, and what lessons from the fact that they almost never see a teacher, or other figure of authority, who is disabled? Many begin to learn that disability matters a great deal in our society, and that disabled people have things done to them by able-bodied people. Being part of an institution designed for the disabled may help to transform disability from something a child has, like red hair, 'O' levels and a penchant for high fashion, into something a child is, an identity that colours the child's entire life.

The strongest evidence for this view comes from the writings of handicapped young people themselves. In *What It's Like to be Me,* Helen Exley (1981, pp.84-5) collected together the views of a large number of handicapped children and young people from many countries. In some of these writings, they reflect on their own social identities:

> I am not my disability, I'm me. I have dyslexia, and I've had polio, but I'm not 'a dyslexic' or 'a cripple'. I'm me.
> *John Swan, 14*

> My ambition is to get out and work somewhere with people who aren't disabled, but I don't know if I could. I will still try. I want to be recognised for what I am — Viviana Ortolan.
> *Viviana Ortolan, 18*

> If you are born handicapped you are labelled from birth. You are sent to special schools, special clubs, special holiday centres. You mix only with other handicapped people. You end up believing you are a lot more handicapped than you are.
> *David Ruebain, 17*

> You see my handicap first and me last.
> *Colleen Henley, 17*

A feature that may become increasingly common in special education in the coming years is the development of special schools catering for a very wide range of children who under pre-1981 legislation would have been placed in separate statutory categories. Those unsympathetic to this development might describe it as the ghetto-ization of special education. Such multi-handicap schools will provide a new range of experiences for children and parents, dictated by the organization of special education rather than by teaching content. In December 1982 it was reported (TES 17 December 1982) that Essex LEA plans to merge an ESN(M) special school with a school for physically handicapped and delicate children. The parents and the LEA saw the proposal in very different ways. The LEA described the merger as 'educationally advisable' on the grounds that a larger school would allow a wider curriculum with more opportunities for staff to specialize. The parents of the physically handicapped children were opposed to the merger on the grounds that the two groups of children should not be mixed. To them these experiences outweighed any benefits gained in teaching content.

Another consequence of schooling that is segregated from the rest of the community is that the friendships that handicapped children establish at school are rarely extended to evenings, weekends and holidays because the catchment area of most special schools is very wide. Mainstream schools put children in touch with others they can befriend, and so help them to be a part of their local community. Special schools, and many special units, force children to stand apart from their community. When children are referred from ordinary to special provision they may lose friendships as a result of loss of daily contact and the common view many people have of special schools as 'daft schools'; the consequences of this process of social exclusion can be profound. (See Radio 1 OU course E241: 'Special Needs in Education'.)

In a study of disabled adolescents Anderson and Clarke (1982, pp. 345-6) found that many young people are not encouraged at school to take part in discussions about their own future, or to develop personal independence:

> The experience of most handicapped children is likely to continually affirm feelings of helplessness. They are deemed to be unable to carry out for themselves many of the daily activities which their non-handicapped peers undertake as of right, and decisions are continually made

about their future by professionals or remote administrators without consulting the young person (or even his family) . . . it is impossible to imagine how the disabled person is to avoid feelings of helplessness if he is not given the basic information to enable him to understand or account for his handicap.

Anderson and Clarke found that schools, both special and ordinary, failed to help children understand their handicap, or to know about their rights to services, and this contributed to the young people's sense of a loss of control over their own lives. One feature of the special curriculum in special schools might be not just the practicalities of living with handicap, but an attempt to help handicapped children to understand their position in society. Children could discuss the kinds of attitudes they are faced with from other children, adults and professionals, the kind of lifestyle they want, and ways to achieve it. In practice, these matters are not on the curriculum agenda and so schools do very little to raise the level of political awareness among their pupils that might enable them to alter their position in society. On the contrary, Anderson and Clarke's evidence suggests that special education operates to keep disabled young people in a weak, dependent position.

Invisible handicap: the other hidden curriculum
If children learn something about handicap from their experience in special schools then ordinary schools provide a mirror-image experience. When handicap and disability are hidden from the gaze of ordinary children and their teachers, this leads to ignorance, to the development of stereotypes and very often, to fear.

In an evaluation of a scheme to integrate children with a wide range of handicaps into a comprehensive school (Ince, Johnstone and Swann, 1983), we sought the views of a sample of teachers in the comprehensive school who taught the handicapped pupils. The initial reactions of a majority were very positive; however, a small number frankly described their unease about physical handicap. One said: 'Basically, I'm not very good with children who are very physically handicapped. I'm very squeamish in a way. I was a bit bothered that I wouldn't be able to cope.' This teacher's view of disabled children was dominated by the notion of a distastful physical appearance, not a surprising view given the fact that she had had virtually no personal experience or knowledge of disabled children or adults before the integration scheme began.

The fear and hostility of some children towards the handicapped are well recognized, and are part of the wider set of social attitudes. Many other children do not display such hostility; yet as a result of segregated education they grow up in ignorance of handicap and they become handicapped themselves by the misconceptions that they may develop. And the attitudes that children develop are not simply a function of the visible handicaps of children with special needs. Children who transfer from ordinary schools to ESN(M) special schools often find themselves the butt of jokes about the 'daft school'. It is the institution, not the child, that is the source of this problem. In our study of an integration scheme in a comprehensive school referred to earlier, the parents of one child reported that their daughter had been called a spastic. This girl was in fact able-bodied, but extremely withdrawn, but she had just come from a special school with many physically handicapped pupils. Her labelling by other children directly resulted from her labelling by the education system.

The promotion of specialism

Much has been written on the subject of educating the deaf and dumb, by gentlemen who have themselves taught and instructed them with great success; and who have been the means, through a bounteous public, of establishing asylums for the exclusive purpose of educating indigent persons of this description. It is to be feared, however, that those establishments have operated like scarecrows with teachers in general, who have been induced, in consequence of the establishment of such asylums, to think there must be so much difficulty in educating these unfortunate mutes, that none are competent to undertake the charge but such as have attended an asylum for instructions, and have thereby acquired a thorough knowledge of all the mysteries of this seemingly occult science. These newly initiated artists, instead of taking off the mask, which was worn by their predecessors, have put another on still more hideous, and thereby dazzled the ignorant with their quackery. (Arrowsmith 1819, pp. 1-2)

In 1819, in his *Art of Instructing the Infant Deaf and Dumb,* John Arrowsmith was well aware of the dangers of professionalizing special education in segregated institutions. People try to justify their separate jobs by creating and promoting specialist activity; their image of expertise dissuades ordinary teachers from being involved; professional territory comes to be defended, and the whole process can become a vicious circle driving special and ordinary education further and further apart.

That many handicapped children need special treatment in order to be successfully educated is beyond question. Debates generally turn on whether or not educators are providing enough of the right kind of special treatment to meet a child's needs. A question less often asked is whether some children receive inappropriately specialized or overspecialized teaching. It is even less often asked how much activity in special schools *is* special.

The ordinary nature of special education
In her report of the Schools Council seminar 'The Curriculum in Special Schools', Mary Wilson (1981) acknowledged that many special schools have more in common with ordinary schools than with each other. In the great majority of special schools most activities are strikingly ordinary. What is unusual is the age range of the children and/or the number of children in the school who are said to be difficult.

Schools for five pre-1981 categories comprise 80 per cent of all special schools. ESN(M) schools are the largest group, with 30 per cent of the total. Tom Wakefield (1977), in an account of the ESN(M) school where he was head, wrote that: 'there were no special methods, just a great deal of extra care.' The amount of time devoted to mastering a task and the staff resources devoted to teaching the children are often unusual; the activity itself seldom is.

Schools for severely mentally handicapped children may strike visitors as exotic, but it is often the unfamiliarity of the children rather than the activities of the school which provoke this response. Much time in many schools is spent on activities closely resembling those in ordinary nursery, infant and junior schools, though the children engaged in them are correspondingly older. Even curricula that appear to be highly specialized, such as that produced by Rectory Paddock School (1981), on closer examination contain only a minority of suggestions for activities that would not occur in ordinary early education. Headings such as 'Memory, Metamemory and Executive Control' can seem exceedingly special, but the activities under the heading are less so:

> The child is asked to reproduce vocally one or more musical notes, sung or played
> The child listens to an audio-tape of sound-effects from, e.g. a kitchen, a farmyard, a classroom etc., and must afterwards describe the scene as he imagines it
> The child is asked to go and tell the secretary that the teacher's phone number is 738691 (Rectory Paddock School 1981, pp. 110-11)

The work that goes beyond the bounds even of nursery education and 'is' identifiably special is the teaching of language and communication, especially in the early stages, and work with children whose developmental level resembles that of ordinary children below the age of two to three.

The third largest category of special school (some 13 per cent of the total) are those for physically handicapped and 'delicate' children. These categories are not educational either by criteria or by consequence. The children so labelled are categorized according to the state of their bodies, although most of their education must depend upon the state of their minds. It is only those aspects of their education directly affected by their disability that are special, such as the use of communication systems like Bliss symbols and the use of hardware like Possum machines. Apart from these, it is very difficult to identify special features of the curriculum in PH schools. In books on the subject (for example, Haskell, Barrett and Taylor, 1977), apart from the heavy stress on medical conditions and problems, one finds little to distinguish curriculum advice from practice in many remedial departments of ordinary schools.

Around 13 per cent of special schools cater for maladjusted children. Many more centres, special classes and units not represented in the statistics of special schools also cater for difficult and disruptive pupils. Once again, the great majority of activities in these places are ordinary. It is frequently claimed that the special feature of these schools is their therapeutic caring environment, however those who try to describe the essential components of such an environment often provide a number of desiderata for teachers and schools in general. For example, Wilson and Evans (1980) give this description of the ideal teacher of the maladjusted:

> An ability to endure in work which was not only very demanding but also often disappointing. . . a reserve of emotional strength and resilience which enabled them to mobilize warm feelings. . . mature. . . did not need to respond primitively and impulsivelyshowed a heightened sensitivity and insight. [Wilson and Evans, 1980, p. 80]

Special features of special education
In stressing the ordinariness of most of special education, I am not asserting that nothing is special, but simply that a small proportion of teaching activities is out of the ordinary. The resources devoted to special schools are very special. In 1981 the cost of special education per pupil was £1,978, compared to £629 per secondary school pupil and £436 per primary school pupil. The major component of this increased cost is the much more favourable staff-pupil ratio of special schools: 7:4 overall in 1981 compared to 16:3 in secondary schools and 22:4 in primary schools (Lukes 1981).

Special levels of resources devoted to ordinary teaching activities are transportable into ordinary schools. However a number of special features of special education are likely to act as barriers to this process. Teachers in special schools do not usually specialize in subject areas or ages of children, but in handicaps. This would be legitimate if the category dictated the special nature of the curriculum, but generally it does not. If the staff currently in special schools were to move into ordinary schools many would, particularly in secondary schools, be faced with an inappropriate specialism or an absence of any appropriate specialism in a system that calls for expertise in subject areas. Logic dictates that if some of the current numbers in special schools are to become part of mainstream classes with support or withdrawal for special teaching, then more ordinary class teachers and subject specialists will be needed. One way to provide this expertise is to retrain teachers in special schools, but at the moment, and for some time to come, there are many ordinary teachers who are already trained and looking for work.

Although much of the work of teachers in special schools is ordinary, they may develop a specialist identity, partly resulting from their training, which encourages them to emphasize whatever is special about the work, and to underestimate the extent to which it could be done by others. The emphasis on therapy in schools for the maladjusted is a good illustration of this process. In a study of a child in a residential school for the maladjusted (Swann, 1982), I found that the atmosphere of the school was far from conducive to personal happiness and good relationships. However children attended daily personal therapy with the deputy head. The headteacher, although he said that 'education was very important' in his school, was primarily concerned with it as a therapeutic environment. At the same time, the school was seriously deficient in many areas of the curriculum. The junior department had for the first time just gained resources to teach subjects other than English, maths and basic art and craft.

The report by HM Inspectorate on educational provision in the ILEA revealed that day schools for the maladjusted had similar problems: 'Schools for the maladjusted have a heavy and desirable investment in psychiatric and psychotherapeutic treatment, but this often dominates their thinking at the expense of curriculum planning. . . standards in some schools, particularly some day schools for the maladjusted, are disturbingly low' (ILEA, 1981, Appendix A, p.3).

In responding to the report, the heads of the schools were

defensive, revealing an important feature of the specialist identity - the belief that only those doing the job have the skills to pass judgement of it. This has considerable implications for the extent to which the professionals are accountable to others. 'We do not feel. . . the report. . . has kept to the standards of clarity and objectivity we would have expected. . .. We are deeply concerned at the damaging impression this must give to those not professionally equipped to evaluate this field of education, especially the parents' (ILEA, 1981, Appendix A, p.3).

The way in which the specialist identity of special school teachers and others whose professional identity is tied to special schools provides a serious barrier to integration is discussed by Patricia Potts in chapter 12 of this book.

Pressures to specialize
One effect of the wider debate about integration that has taken place since the Warnock Report is that special schools have come under greater pressure to identify their special contribution. The sense of threat is made clear by Mittler (1979) when he writes: 'special schools [for the mentally handicapped] will really need to become specialized centres of excellence rather than isolated havens of care if they are to continue to justify their existence in the face of mounting pressures towards more integrated forms of provision' (Mittler, 1979, p.190). Many recent writings on the special curriculum are aimed at giving special schools a common special identity, although the benefit of this line of development for individual children is seldom clear. Despite Wilson's recognition of the many common features of special and ordinary schools, her report of the Schools Council seminar emphasized a need to strengthen the common characteristics of special school curricula: '. . .planning for pupils with diverse needs is not a new experience in special schools. What is relatively new is a realization of the value of a framework for the total curriculum into which modifications for particular pupils or groups can be fitted without loss of coherence' (Wilson 1981, p. 10).

Behaviourism in special education

The behavioural objectives approach to special education provides an example of an attempt to create a specialist curriculum, as well as a limited view of the curriculum as a set of teacher-devised plans. Despite its rapid growth in popularity I shall argue against the all-pervasive use of this approach and suggest that it has a much more limited application than many people assume.

The growth of behavioural objectives

The use of behavioural objectives became popular in mainstream education in America in the 1950s and the approach continues to be extensively used (Tyler, 1949; Mager 1962), though curricula based on behavioural objectives have not attained the same degree of popularity in British mainstream education. In special education, the approach was advocated in the first instance for use in schools for mentally handicapped children following the transfer of this group from health to education in 1971 (1974 in Scotland). Probably the most important influence in this process has been the Hester Adrian Research Centre and its associated projects, including the Schools Council Project on Teaching Language and Communication to the mentally handicapped (Leeming et al. 1979); the Education of the Developmentally Young (EDY) Project (McBrien 1981) and the Teaching and the Severely Subnormal (TASS) Project (Robson 1981). LEA educational psychologists and advisers have promoted these projects in many schools. In the late 1970s, the promotion of behavioural objectives expanded into the ESN(M) field. The approach was most thoroughly presented by Ainscow and Tweddle (1979).

However, curricula based on behavioural objectives have come to be advocated for the whole of special education. The Warnock Report defined the curriculum as follows:

> There are four interrelated elements which contribute to the development of a curriculum. They are: (i) setting of objectives; (ii) choice of materials and experiences; (iii) choice of teaching and learning methods to attain the objectives; and (iv) appraisal of appropriateness of the

objectives and the effectiveness of the means of achieving them. (DES, 1978, p.206)

Here the objectives approach is recommended for special education in general, as it is by Mittler (1981) who listed the skills and knowledge that all special educators need; as one of their core skills they must 'have proficiency in the specification of behavioural objectives, goal setting, task analysis, programme writing. . .' Ainscow and Tweddle, as well, linked the special nature of special schools directly to the use of behavioural objectives:

> We will. . . proceed on the assumption that they are special schools because sophisticated teaching methods and techniques are used in them. . . . In fact, it [the behavioural objectives approach] is the kind of system which should be operated in a special school or unit if it is 'special' in more than name only. (Ainscow and Tweddle 1979, p.105)

It is likely that the approach will be further boosted by the introduction of statements of special educational needs under the 1981 Education Act. In order to avoid identifying special treatment as a special place, those writing the statement will try to specify the nature of the child's programme. Objectives plans will almost certainly be the result. This development has a ready-made model in the American Individualized Educational Plan (IEP) which by law must list objectives for the child (see Booth, 1982).

From an approach developed with severely mentally handicapped children in mind, curricula based on behavioural objectives have expanded to encompass all of special education, including the provision of special education within ordinary schools. The assumption has been made by a number of writers that the behavioural approach is the essence of special education.

Are behavioural objectives a special case?
What are the grounds for the claim that the behavioural approach is particularly appropriate to teaching children with

special needs? In most respects, the use of behavioural methods is not particular to special education. Behavioural objectives can be, have been, and are used with children at all levels of ability both in and out of special education. Although the actual objectives set may be special, the process of setting objectives itself does not mark out any special activity of use only or even mainly in special education. On the contrary, the application of behavioural objectives and companion approaches such as precision teaching in special schools post-dates its use in ordinary schools by many years.

In response to this, it is commonly asserted that while they do have general application, behavioural objectives are especially important for children with learning difficulties, because these children do not learn 'incidentally' or 'spontaneously'; they require highly structured and planned learning experiences. It is often claimed of severely mentally handicapped children, in terms like this: 'Research findings support a structured approach. Evidence from a number of sources indicates that the mentally handicapped do not learn spontaneously from a stimulating environment. An enrichment approach, therefore, is unlikely to be effective' (Crawford 1980, p.11).

But the idea is used to justify teaching with tightly defined behavioural objectives at all levels of learning difficulty (see Neville Hallmark, chapter 10). It found its way, for example, into an interim report of the Schools Council's project on Health Education for Slow Learners: 'The less able do not learn easily from incidental situations. The project therefore made an attempt to put together a structured approach with topics repeated at regular stages. . .' (Schools Council/Health Education Council, 1982).

The idea that children with learning difficulties have a deficit of incidental or spontaneous learning that justifies a particular approach to their education deserves critical examination. Whether a particular child has difficulties in learning a particular task will depend on the performance of that child, not on a generalization derived from research. It is also difficult to know what spontaneous learning could possibly mean. Something spontaneous, like spontaneous combustion, happens without an external stimulus. Learning, by definition, involves external stimulation. 'Spontaneous learning' is, therefore, a contradiction in terms. No one learns spontaneously.

The claim that children with learning difficulties have an 'incidental learning deficit' is not much easier to comprehend. Doing something incidentally means doing something that is not part of one's current purpose. In order to make any sense of the claim that the less able do not learn easily from incidental situations we need to ask: 'What is it they do not learn easily, incidental to what activity?' Perhaps the 'incidental learning deficit' simply means that these children learn very slowly. Yet there is no reason logically to argue that the rate at which a child learns should determine the teaching methods used. Of course, precisely this point of view is argued by many; the slower a child learns the more 'structured' the teaching has to be:

> The educational approach adopted in this book may fairly be described as 'structured', in that it is based upon systematic programmes of learning (behavioural) objectives. The reason for this is the obvious one that mentally handicapped children find learning very difficult, and anyone who is confronted by learning tasks which they find difficult will need a structured approach if they are to succeed. (Rectory Paddock School 1981, p.10)

There are two false moves in this argument. The first is to suppose that some teaching is unstructured, whereas in fact all teaching has a structure of some kind. The second is to equate structure with the use of behavioural objectives. The resulting claim that learning difficult tasks requires programmes of objectives is surprising in view of the fact that most things learnt by most people, whether easy or difficult, never involve teaching by objectives. Moreover, if the claim that mentally handicapped children need highly structured teaching in order to learn were true, one would not expect them to learn anything outside such situations. Yet mentally handicapped children do learn a great deal in informal settings where no objectives are specified.

Behavioural objectives and curricular relevance

The process of specifying behavioural objectives is no guarantee of appropriate teaching; indeed the illustrations of content in writings on behavioural objectives bear some study. Ainscow and Tweddle (1979) have written the most thorough British exposition of the approach as applied to children with learning difficulties, and they base their case for its adoption on teacher effectiveness: 'Experience of in-service training for teachers in both primary and special schools fully confirms our belief that giving teachers skills of writing objectives and encouraging them to do so before planning teaching methods significantly increases the probability that the objectives will in fact be achieved' (Ainscow and Tweddle 1979, p.21).

In support of their case Ainscow and Tweddle quote Lewis Carroll's Cheshire Cat:

> Alice asked the Cheshire Cat:
> 'Would you tell me please, which way I ought to go from here?'
> 'That depends a good deal on where you want to go', said the Cat.
> 'I don't much care where. . .', said Alice.
> 'Then it doesn't matter which way you go', said the Cat.

One should perhaps use this source with caution, since just after this exchange, the Cheshire Cat declares that he is mad. One view of the dialogue is that Alice is asking for a moral directive which the Cheshire Cat reduces to a matter of Alice's personal desires – a morality that would be difficult to sustain outside Wonderland, but one that comes uncomfortably close to the reality of teaching by objectives. The central problem with the approach is that it is advocated as a curriculum, but in fact it is not. The important questions of what should be taught and why do not form part of the formal process of specifying objectives. The specification of objectives is no guarantee that teaching will be appropriate. This can be illustrated by some of the example programmes Ainscow and Tweddle provide and what they say about their use. Take the following two objectives: 'States 2 things that can be bought at the bakers (bread and cakes). States 2 ingredients of bread (yeast and flour).' Are these good or bad objectives? This question is not considered. Instead the authors give a list of points to check before using them, preceded by the statement: 'we will assume that the subject area selected reflects the child's priority educational need, and that one of the teaching goals is appropriate for the pupil in question.' The problem of just what is appropriate is not confronted, and there follows a list of technical considerations such as: 'Do you agree with the sequence or order of objectives?' and 'Is the step-size appropriate?'

However one should not be led to assume that no theory guides the choice of examples or that they are a random selection. In fact these two objectives typify a number of characteristics of all the language programmes mentioned in the book. They require *responsive* language: that children might need to ask questions or issue directions is never mentioned. They require *decontextualized* language: words are taken out of their formal contexts – sentences and phrases – and out of their functional contexts – buying things in shops. But the most significant effect of such objectives is to remove them from the needs, interests and experience of individual children. These two particular objectives come from a programme said to be a 'popular approach in areas of social disadvantage where a relatively high proportion of children may have retarded language development'. It is hard to see what use to children from run-down inner-city areas there could be in knowing two ingredients of bread, as an isolated chunk of knowledge. The programme runs the risk of being restrictive and irrelevant, largely because so little attention is devoted to simple but important questions of value: what kind of experience do we want to give children, and to what end?

The range of application of the approach
It is very frustrating to teach a child over a long period and to see little progress as a result. So a method that makes visible change more likely is immediately attractive. For some simple skills like using the toilet, tying up shoelaces and using a knife and fork, programmes of behavioural objectives may be legitimately applied. But many other abilities cannot be

reduced to the acquisition of skills in this way. In teaching children to talk, to reason, to discuss, we aim to develop their understanding. Their behaviour is no more than an indication of that understanding, and the links between behaviour and understanding are frequently complex and unclear. It is easy to be misled by a simple change in behaviour to suppose that it means something more.

An increasingly common approach to teaching severely mentally handicapped children is to derive teaching programmes from research on the cognitive development of normal children. Psychologists study children in experiments in order to discover what they have achieved at any given stage. For example, Piaget tested children's understanding of the permanence of objects by seeing if they tried to retrieve objects when they were hidden from view. The development of this understanding is delayed in mentally handicapped children. Kiernan, Jordan and Saunders (1978) suggested that 'teaching object permanence should be straightforward' by turning the experiment which tests the ability into a teaching task. Yet to suppose that a severely mentally handicapped child who had been taught to retrieve a hidden object had the same understanding as a normal child would be quite erroneous. The achievement of object permanence is the result of 12 to 18 months of experience for a normal child. This lengthy process of interaction and example cannot be bypassed, indeed it seems reasonable to claim that a mentally handicapped child would need much more such experience to achieve comparable understanding. Thus the effectiveness of behavioural change can be properly assessed only by asking what a particular behaviour indicates about a child's understanding.

Behavioural objectives and integration
I suggested earlier that the growth of the behavioural objectives approach is partly the result of the pressure on special schools to justify their existence. The approach directs attention towards a small part of children's experiences at school, and away from many potent effects of segregation. Yet a contrasting view is taken by many, namely that the use of behavioural objectives actually promotes integration by enabling teachers to identify very precisely the way in which a

child is 'failing' in learning or behaviour in ordinary school, and to correct the problem. Coventry are employing this programme in their 'Special Needs Action Programme' (SNAP) of in-service training for primary school teachers. It aims to help teachers identify and help children at risk of failure by devising precise teaching programmes of behavioural objectives. The period of help is seen as a temporary support before children reintegrate into the mainstream.

But can such efforts promote integration? The approach assumes that it is the children rather than the curricula which need a remedy. The mainstream curriculum that did not meet the needs of the children in the first place remains unchallenged and so the generating force for segregation remains the same. Secondly it is not linked to an LEA policy for integration of children currently in special schools. Resources that could be used to meet the needs of children with learning difficulties in the mainstream continue to be tied up in special schools. Coventry has a highly developed special school sector and the SNAP programme has been implemented before any clear plans have been published for the future of special schools. A senior officer in Coventry has remarked that ordinary schools should be helped to meet the needs of the existing 20 per cent of children in mainstream schools who have learning difficulties before the LEA contemplates introducing children currently in special schools. So although SNAP, and programmes like it, may stem the tide of special school referrals, it will not, on its own, reverse the process of segregation that has already taken place. Thirdly, an almost inevitable consequence of behavioural objectives programmes in the mainstream is that they concentrate on basic skills. Not only is the child segregated from his peers by the way he is taught, he is also given a reduced curriculum. Finally, behavioural objectives programmes involve an extreme form of individualized teaching. In a highly individualized curriculum there is little room for learning co-operatively, for sharing knowledge, for children teaching each other. Knowledge is treated as a commodity dispensed by a teacher to individuals, who use it to progress through the curriculum. Under these circumstances, children have little or no responsibility towards each other.

It has been argued that the use of behavioural objectives will facilitate teacher accountability and this itself may have implications for integration. Ainscow and Tweddle (1979, p.142) have taken this position:

> ... it is generally agreed that for accountability to become a reality, three important conditions must exist:
> 1   There must be a programme of objectives, defined in behavioural terms, and including details of performance levels;
> 2   The programme must be understood as far as possible, by everybody concerned;
> 3   It must be clear to everybody concerned what everybody else is to do in terms of producing and operating the programme (i.e. role specification).

However, if everyone's greatest effort is invested in attaining individual objectives, there will be little stress on children of different abilities sharing a common curriculum. There would be pressure to make children with learning difficulties the responsibility of specialist teachers, in order to minimize the risk of mainstream teachers being held accountable for the failure of slow-learning children. In a rigidly accountable system the tendency is towards homogeneous teaching groups, limited and strictly defined responsibilities for teachers, and segregation across the ability range.

In sum, although there may be short-term gains from the use of behavioural objectives programmes to prevent referral to special schools, there are strong grounds for arguing that the approach offers more opportunities for a process of segregation than for the reverse.

Concluding remarks: steps to an integrated curriculum

In this chapter, I have offered a critique of current thinking on the special curriculum, and have argued that it is not designed to foster integration. In conclusion, I shall describe some of the principles on which an alternative approach might develop which contributes to the process of increasing participation of children with special needs in the mainstream. These are intended as a contribution to a project shared between many chapters in this book.

The curriculum should be concerned to develop a community in which handicapped people can participate at all levels and in all spheres of life. We may succeed in teaching handicapped children the skills that will help them to be independent, but their future independence also relies on other pleople allowing them the resources to use those skills. One of the goals of schooling should be the elimination of prejudice against handicap as well as racism and sexism from the curriculum.

The prerequisite for the elimination of prejudice is knowledge arising from day-to-day contact. However it is important to avoid the patronage of handicapped children by others. In order to break down barriers, one comprehensive school which had begun to integrate some physically handicapped children established a scheme which paired volunteers among the mainstream children with children at the local special school from which the integrated children had come. The mainstream children visited the special school, not vice versa, and the handicapped children were not consulted as to whether they wished to participate. Although the contacts were beneficial and some friendships were established, the children did not meet on equal terms.

Anderson (1973) compared the concerns of junior school class teachers who were just about to receive a physically handicapped child into their class with their attitudes after one term. The proportion who were a little or considerably worried fell in this time from 43 to 7 per cent. Most concerns related to whether the child, and the teacher, would cope. A typical comment was the following: 'It was my first teaching post and I was on probation. I wasn't sure generally how I'd cope, or what the reactions of the other children would be.' It appears from Anderson's results that straightforward exposure to the children, coupled with accurate and useful information, is important in dispelling these fears. This is confirmed by Hegarty and Pocklington (1981b), who also found that the frequently negative or hostile reactions amongst teachers gradually gave way to more positive and accepting views.

In addition to the normal contact that arises from

handicapped and ordinary children being educated together, schools should consider including the study of disability and handicap as part of the curriculum. This could be done at many levels, ranging from components of community or general studies courses to CSE or 'O' level courses. Pupils could investigate local resources for disabled people; disabled people could teach children as part of the course.

Schools and teachers themselves need to examine their own attitudes and prejudices. It is naive to assume that children's attitudes will change without a commensurate change in staff attitudes. In this sense, the school as a whole community should work together, since it may be that the staff need to change more than the pupils. As part of this process, there should be attempts to encourage handicapped people to work in schools.

The central task of curriculum development should be to make the mainstream curriculum accessible to a wider range of children. As a strategy for curriculum development schools need to begin not with the children who fail, but with a close examination of their existing curricula. Making the curriculum accessible entails changes in school organization, so that individual timetables can be prepared, groupings can be flexible and support staff can move around between lessons and departments according to need. In revising curriculum materials, accessibility should not simply mean adapting existing materials. It will also entail new material that will bring teaching closer to the interests and background knowledge of the children. None of these tasks can be seen as the job of specialist teachers alone. They require commitment from mainstream teachers to extend and develop their work. The specialist may then work in collaboration, providing extra resources and knowledge.

An important component of making the curriculum accessible should be the development of closer links between the school and the community. This involves not just opening the school up to the community to use its resources in the evenings and at weekends, but also exploiting the resources of the community to expand the school's own activities. Particularly at a time of high unemployment there is a vast pool of expertise that could be harnessed which would have the effect of making schools less remote from the rest of children's lives. David Hargreaves (1981) has argued that the core of the secondary curriculum should be an integrated course of community studies aimed at developing the children's critical understanding of their environment.

Finally, curriculum development must be seen as part of a wider policy for integration. The beginning of such an approach can be seen for remedial education in Grampian, described by Tony Booth (chapter 3). Here the resources were allocated so that it was feasible for schools, individually and in areas, to develop resource centres and new curricula to give access to more children with learning difficulties. The teaching practices and the policy framework developed in a consistent way. Without this close relationship, curriculum development either cannot be sustained, or it may work directly to counter its apparent intentions.

8
Providing Access to the Mainstream Curriculum in Secondary Schools

JEAN GARNETT

Introduction

The concept of special educational need, as defined in the Warnock Report, refers not only to those children with identifiable disabilities but also to a much wider group which includes all children with learning difficulties in ordinary schools. The concept encourages the notion of a continuum of need rather than a series of pigeonholes into which children have so far been uncomfortably and often inappropriately slotted. It focuses attention on common factors and 'degrees' of need rather than on differences and 'kind' of child, and to encompasses at least a fifth of our school population.

Such a radical change of emphasis demands an equally radical change of attitude across an education system steeped in a tradition of selection and categorization, and in the acceptance of a separate system for a special but significant minority for whom an ordinary curriculum has been thought to be inaccessible. In the light of this change the aim of this chapter is to consider some of the factors that I have identified during my experience first, of developing special needs departments in three comprehensive schools in Oxfordshire and Nottinghamshire, and then in the advisory field in Coventry where some 21 comprehensive schools are offered support, both for the developments of their provision to meet special educational needs and for in-service teacher training.

Two major strands run through the discussion. The first is concerned with the evolutionary nature of the task, with the need to start at the point where attitudes and school ethos can accommodate change, and develop from there. The second strand considers the problem of making the mainstream curriculum accessible to pupils with special needs and what implications this has for organization within schools.

Coordinating provision for pupils with special needs

My first experience of running a special unit for ESN(M) pupils, attached to Bicester Comprehensive School, lasted some five years, during which time the unit gradually moved into the centre of the main site to become the school's resource for meeting all special needs emerging from its pupil population (Garnett 1976). From being educated quite separately the unit pupils were slowly integrated into mainstream classes when it seemed sensible to do so. The process was a result of increasing unease on the part of the staff about educating one group of children separately from others in a school that was aiming to be truly comprehensive. Along with the general trend in Oxfordshire at the time, we were concerned primarily with the physical, then the organizational, problems of integrating pupils with special needs and the subsequent changes in the unit's supportive role. It was only later that we began to address ourselves to the implications of the process for the mainstream curriculum.

It was at the Cooper School, Bicester, that the idea of a co-ordinator for special needs was born. My major task as this co-ordinator was to link the special unit with the remedial department and the mainstream with regard to placing the pupils with learning difficulties, to make sure of curriculum consistency for those pupils, and to provide a point of reference for such external services as child guidance, schools psychological service and social services, bringing together pupil, parents and professionals as needs arose. Children with behaviour difficulties were also referred to the co-ordinator, who had responsibility for helping staff to find strategies for meeting the children's particular needs, but not for providing long-term alternative provision.

The aim was to offer an emergency 'time-out' facility with the co-ordinator, which meant that teachers could have a much needed short respite from the pressure but were not able to abdicate completely their responsibility for searching for ways to cope with their pupils' difficulties. We found that what teachers need most was immediate support during crises, time to allow their anger and frustration to subside and meanwhile be able to put their heads together with a specialist to find a way through the problem. Staff then began to cope much better with those children who created disturbances which were out of all proportion to the general behavioural difficulties experienced in the ordinary way of school life.

For the pupils, the time with the co-ordinator could be used to look quietly at the problem and to bring them to the point where they were able to take a step forward in improving their behaviour and relationships with the teachers involved and in school generally.

At that time the trend towards removing the artificial distinctions between handicapped and non-handicapped was beginning to gain momentum, but interestingly the Cooper School maintained separate provision for the 'ESN(M)' and 'remedial' pupils (each of these departments having its own head), although it was difficult to see where the curricula offered to the two groups differed. However, when the pupils attended mainstream lessons – often supported by either the 'special' or 'remedial' teachers – they were taught from the same syllabus as the mainstream pupils, and they all belonged to mainstream tutor groups. This kind of paradox does not seem to be uncommon.

Traditional remedial departments often appear to see the attachment of a special unit as a threat to their own position in the school. They do not generally view themselves as 'special educators' although they are likely to defend the notion that their pupils usually require a different kind of curriculum from those in the mainstream. That difference is not clearly defined but the adapted curriculum is certainly narrower. The pupils are identified as 'slow learners' but not 'handicapped'. The latter children are thought to need yet another kind of curriculum. The fact that in essence the curricula observed to be offered in the different settings seem to be little different in terms of their aims, objectives and content is not always recognized.

Similar attitudes appear to prevail amongst many

mainstream teachers, who tend to view the educational needs of children with learning difficulties as being outside their province and so the responsibility of the remedial or special teachers. The more handicapped the child the more uncertain are the teachers about their own capabilities to meet his needs. However, overwhelming evidence from a variety of educational settings shows that the diet being offered to low achievers in the mainstream and to children in remedial and special departments is not meeting their learning needs effectively, and that teachers are becoming uncomfortably aware of an urgent need for change. It is through this developing awareness that I see opportunities for positive progress in the integration process if we can but take them up.

The Nottinghamshire school, numbering about 2,000 on roll and set in the tough mining area in the north of the county, was strictly streamed across a 14-form intake, and its special courses department ran as a separate entity for the bottom two special classes in each year group, with remedial classes 'blocked' for their basic subjects further up. Here I met the school-within-a-school pattern typical of many of the examples of integration described in Hegarty and Pocklington (1982). Again there was a distinction between 'special' and 'remedial' and again it is difficult to ascertain the difference in curriculum objectives and practice between the one and the other.

It seemed to me and other colleagues that the separateness of the special classes did little to help the pupils to integrate into a normal world. In fact we felt the system to be quite divisive and we met a high level of behaviour disorder and disruption, particularly among the older special class groups. In general their self-respect and expectations were low: I remember Gary, a bright, provocative, argumentative and very eloquent boy saying, 'We must be thick, else why are we in this class?'

We set about opening up the unit and the next year all first-year special and remedial pupils were placed in mixed-ability tutor groups, the special pupils being taught in the special unit for their basic subjects only.

This one move had a considerable effect on the mainstream staff, who found themselves having to teach our pupils for some of the time. I learned from the problems we had to work through then that change could be achieved only as fast as the attitudes, relationships and coping capacities of colleagues would allow. It seems that ordinary and special teachers alike can become increasingly confused about their several roles and responsibilities. Confusion and uncertainty tend to lead to entrenchment, which may be the most difficult obstacle encountered by teachers involved in the process of integration. Seamus Hegarty argues that rather than increasing the problem for ordinary schools, the integration process can have a major influence on them, acting as 'a stimulus for examining its [the school's] goals and objectives and developing its educational provision so as to cater more appropriately for all its pupils' (Hegarty 1982). He suggests that the process can bring about fundamental changes in a school's whole policy and practice and forces the question: 'What are schools for?'

If this is the case, the future role of the school's special educators will be crucial to the whole school's way of life and not just to that of a special group. Those involved in the preparation of a special needs department will have this in mind as they set about their tasks. They will recognize that although secondary schools have curricular and organizational similarities, each is unique in terms of its catchment area, its philosophies, policy and ethos. A range of curriculum organizations, of streaming, banding, setting and mixed-ability permutations exists and pastoral organization may be vertical or horizontal. Special teaching may take place in special or remedial classes, extraction or withdrawal groups or in mixed-ability settings with the special teachers supporting the mainstream classes, or any combination of these.

What does seem to be common is the trend to increase the amount of time that children with special needs spend in mainstream classes or with mainstream teachers; this frequently now amounts to 50 per cent or more of their school time. What preparations have been made to accommodate this situation so far? You only have to follow a child with special needs through a normal school day to see that this is a nettle that needs to be grasped urgently.

In all three schools it was the headteachers' attitude and their awareness of the school's responsibilities to pupils with special needs that carried the greatest influence. Most important was the recognition that:

1 around a fifth of the pupils are likely to need special help during some, or all of their time in the school;
2 such a proportion requires an appropriate share of teacher time and resources;
3 the person responsible for developing the special needs department needs to carry some authority and this has implications for the salary scale of the post. As a scale 3 head of progress unit I carried little influence beyond the confines of the unit itself and less credibility when trying to promote in-service initiatives. As a scale 4 co-ordinator and later a senior teacher head of special education courses, it was accepted – no, expected – that there should be the capacity and expertise for both;
4 all teachers in the school have some responsibility for meeting the learning needs of all the pupils they teach, including those with special difficulties; the task of the special educators is not to relieve their mainstream colleagues entirely of that responsibility but to provide a resource to support them and their pupils in whatever ways are appropriate.

The co-ordinator's role

I have tried to devise a pattern for co-ordinating special needs in the comprehensive school, – influenced by McCall's three models (McCall 1980) – that might act as a point of reference for those responsible for developing departments of special needs. The most important criterion in the pattern's formation was that it had to be adaptable to every kind of school organization.

The role and responsibilities of a co-ordinator for special educational needs in a secondary school can be grouped into three major areas:

1 *Identification* of all pupils with special needs in co-operation with other senior staff: deputy head, year head, house head and heads of departments.

2 *Management* of a special resource base, set in the centre of the school, which acts as the 'hub' of the support service. The base is organized to meet whatever special needs emerge in that school. Its functions are not too precisely defined so that it can be flexible to the changing needs of the school. This leaves options open to support a variety of forms of organization.

3 *Support/advice* within the mainstream curriculum.

   (a) Departmental 'key' teachers are appointed to liaise with the co-ordinator about making the mainstream curriculum accessible to pupils with special needs.

   (b) 'Key' teachers act as departmental heads.

   (c) Special teachers support mainstream teachers within the classroom where appropriate.

The Coventry remedial service

Coventry's remedial education service is based at the city's teachers' centre from where it aims to support all teachers with special needs pupils in their classes, wherever they may be – special, primary or secondary schools, or a special remedial or mainstream class. In the primary sector the concept of the co-ordinator is being developed through an extensive in-service training programme. Some secondary schools are taking up the notion as they reorganize to accommodate both falling rolls and the 14 to 19 initiative which is being put into effect across the city as its response to the high local unemployment problem and the growing educational demands of 16 to 19-year-olds (*Times Educational Supplement,* 9 July 1982).

One school decided recently to dispense with its special class system in the first three years and put all the special pupils into mainstream classes. This threw both the remedial and ordinary staff into turmoil, as might be expected, and nobody knew quite how to start. However, with advisory support things began to sort themselves out. The remedial teachers were helped to reorganize their rooms as a resource/learning centre and the English department appointed a 'key' teacher to have responsibility for curriculum development for meeting special needs in English classes. The head of remedial, helped by the teacher/adviser, tested all first- to third-year pupils to find out who would need extensive teaching in the learning centre, who needed help with specific problems like spelling and who had individual difficulties to which their English teacher should be alerted. Each remedial teacher was timetabled to support each English teacher for one lesson across years 1 to 3. (The school continues to provide an alternative curriculum for special pupils in years 4 and 5.) As teething troubles were overcome, a similar operation was planned to take place with the maths department and so gradually through the other disciplines.

The success of such ventures seems to depend on:

1 teachers' (special and mainstream) determination to make it work;
2 the willingness of mainstream staff to allow the special teachers into their classrooms and make use of their skills;
3 the capacity of the head of special education to readjust himself to the demands of the policy change; his organizational skill, and sensitivity to teachers' as well as pupils' needs;
4 the capacity of everyone to adjust the mainstream curriculum to make it accessible to the broader group. This requires critical observation and a willingness to make further changes when problems arise;
5 effective in-service initiatives in co-operation with the advisory service to facilitate these changes;
6 continuing advisory support to help with the inevitable obstacles.

The mainstream curriculum

I have considered the features of the school which affect the development of provision for children with special needs and have concentrated on the attitudes of staff, the organization of the school and the quality and autonomy of the person responsible for co-ordinating the provision. But the extent to which the mainstream curriculum can be made accessible to pupils with special needs is also fundamental. If, in most schools, children with special needs spend at least half their time in mainstream classes, then for this reason alone, we have to attend to two questions. How can the curriculum in the school be made accessible to pupils with special needs? What implications does this have for the way the school is organized as a whole?

Special and remedial teachers have in the past opted for an alternative curriculum, running parallel to that operating in the mainstream, believing that their children are not able to learn from a mainstream curriculum. Yet for years it has been the remedial teachers' stated aim to return as many as possible to normal classes. But the longer a child remains in this separated situation, the poorer are his chances of catching up if and when he does return, and it is therefore not surprising that few do actually make the mainstream and that their progress once they get there is generally limited.

Various excursions into curriculum planning have led me to believe that special education pupils can learn effectively from a mainstream curriculum given that: teacher attitudes favour it; the learning objectives are appropriately set and teaching strategies and methods are geared to meet them; incentives for learning are incorporated and are seen to work; and classroom organization and planning take into account the *individual* learning needs of *all* the class members. By incentives I mean addressing ourselves to the immense variety of rewarding experiences, both external and internal, that spark off children's learning. Behaviour modification techniques might be relevant as a vehicle for attaining more fundamental incentives. They are not an end in themselves.

Several teachers in Coventry schools are working to devise curricula for pupils by analysing the tasks involved in teaching a subject area.

The principle, by no means original, is that the subject matter is analysed for the concepts involved and the contexts in which they are met. The skills needed for the pupils to understand the subject matter are also identified and taught where necessary.

The model was first tried out by Catherine Hunter, a probationer history teacher who came to the remedial centre, in some distress, seeking help to find a way to 'get through' to a difficult class of second-year 'B' band pupils. She stated that

Chapter	Ideas/concepts	Reference material	Group activity skills	Personal learning	Study skills	Specific learning
1 2	Peer groups/gangs Trespassing Hero-worship	'Street gang' by Webster (Here Today) Extract from 'The Otterbury Incident' by C. Day Lewis 'Sad Story of Lefty and Ned' (Billy the Kid)	Group discussion Reporting back Group writing	Retelling personal experiences Writing own poetry	Dictionary work Listening	Spelling: cigarettes Blank verse Rhyming verse Rhythm in poetry Adverbs
3	Gossip–distortion Psychology of being disabled	Pages 18, 19, 20 Billy Griffiths Wingy Oliver	'Class whisper'	Writing a business letter to agency concerned with the disabled	Researching polio Library skills Note-making	Punctuation of letter Using an index
4	Bias in reporting Deprivation	'The Whole Truth?' – Soccer unit 'Timothy Winters'	Group discussion Role play – case conference on 'Suzie'	Writing, biased report of own sporting event	Distinguishing 'fact' from opinion	Comprehension Vocabulary: vehement alternative territorial simulated flattering Cliché–jargon
	Attitudes to the police	Pages 32 – 4	Class discussion	Write three views of Rocky's arrest	Finding evidence of bias or prejudice in reports	
5	Qualities of leadership Territorial sense	Description of the meeting place – gang hideout	Paired discussion	Ordering priorities Writing about 'discussed' hideout	Writing a list	Handwriting

Figure 1 *A Pair of Jesus-Boots* by Sylvia Sherry

they were uninterested, not learning and behaving badly. The plan she devised is set out in figure 1. Later she grouped her pupils for separate activities and they later reported back to the rest of the class. After that she identified for each pupil the group learning skills he/she needed to develop. By adapting the model to meet her purposes she had:

1 analysed the content of the material;
2 identified the group activity skills, study skills and mastery skills required for her pupils to learn more efficiently;
3 set target objectives for certain learning areas;
4 organized the class according to the requirements of the activity;
5 and in so doing encouraged the pupils to learn because they understood what was being asked of them.

She returned three weeks later to report that things were improving: the pupils were better behaved and seemed to be learning more.

Since then other teachers working with this model have observed that a wider group of pupils are working harder, writing more coherently and behaving better, while those with difficulties seem to have a stronger grasp of the material. These observations have given us some indication that the exercise is worth pursuing and also that evaluation and assessment need to be given attention. Trials of this kind demand that we record what we are doing, how we are doing it, what progress is being made and the modification being effected.

Arthur Parsons, an experienced English teacher who has analysed part of his course in accordance with the principles of this model (see figure 1), observes that:

1 it clarified what was to be taught and I was clearer about where I was going with the programme;
2 it highlighted over-repetition in teaching modes and practices;
3 it pointed up omissions in learning/study skills teaching;
4 more efficient definition of particular study/mastery skills emerged from it;

5 it showed a need for actual teaching of group activity
   skills;
6 it led to a means of assessing individual pupils' progress

The head of another school's support services works
alongside departmental heads to adapt their curricula for the
special pupils. For instance, the science department now has
two parallel booklets on the various themes, one a simplified
version of the other but under identical covers. All pupils are
free to choose either. It is observed that most select the
appropriate level.

To support the skills area of the model, an 'Items for
Learning' sheet has been designed for teachers to record
specific learning objectives for individual pupils. These are
identified through the reading and marking of the pupils'
written work. The sheet is placed at the back of the pupil's
exercise book and can help to link learning in a mainstream
class with that in the child's special class.

The difference between this sort of record and others is that
it lays out the objectives to be *achieved* not items that have been
covered. It can be operated in a variety of ways either for pupils
with special needs only or for the whole class. Used for the
whole class it can be instrumental in doing away with the
stigma that develops when children are singled out for special
attention, since every member of the class is singled out each
for his own particular learning needs.

The learning objectives, identified during the marking of the
assignment in question, are written in an 'Items for Learning'
column, the dates for when the item was started, mastered and
checked are recorded as an important guide to the rate at which
learning is taking place. Dating the start and achievement
points also provides the pupil and teacher with a means of
assessing progress. There are, furthermore, implications for
classroom planning because pupils can be grouped for similar
learning items.

Arthur Parsons decided to operate this record for all the
pupils in his mixed-ability class and observed that it: eased his
marking task; provided pupils with the incentive to solve their
own learning problems; pointed a way to individualize learning

(and was useful in providing homework tasks); and worked as well for 'high fliers' as for those with learning difficulties.

Conclusion

It is becoming increasingly evident that when special and ordinary teachers begin to work together on finding ways into the mainstream curriculum for children with learning difficulties, interesting things happen to the teachers as well as to the curriculum. They discover that: the special pupils' needs and difficulties are not all that different from those of others; there is no mystique attached to the special teacher's task, just careful and ordered planning and teaching; teachers have a great deal to learn from each other, which may benefit all the children. Most important, the special teachers are made aware of the need to work *within* the context of the mainstream curriculum rather than outside it. Where the children are taught – special classroom, ordinary class or tutorial setting – may become less of an issue.

The impact of all this on the organization of the department of special needs is self-evident. It means that although a department may start off as a traditional, separate entity, it is possible to effect organizational change via the mainstream curriculum, which is already probably being offered to most of the department's children.

9
Resources for Meeting Special Needs in Secondary Schools

ELIZABETH JONES

Introduction

This chapter seeks to outline a model for resourcing comprehensive schools in response to the special educational needs of pupils. Its starting point is that there should be a curriculum accessible to all pupils, a principle that is at the heart of comprehensive education but which is not yet common practice.

Since the Education Act of 1944, when the overall figure of need for 'special educational treatment' was estimated at 17 per cent, most such special educational treatment has been provided in ordinary schools, which have attempted to meet the needs of many children with learning difficulties, particularly in the areas of literacy and numeracy. The arrangements that most schools made, independent of LEA initiatives or policymaking, came to be called 'remedial' provision, taking the form either of separate departments and classes or of withdrawal from mainstream lessons. But there was always uncertainty about remedial education. Was it the provision of an alternative curriculum? Or was it the remediation of learning difficulties so that pupils would be able to participate in the mainstream curriculum?

A special curriculum?

If one asks what is special about this specialist provision most schools point with a degree of satisfaction to those individuals and *small groups* who are regularly withdrawn from 'normal' classrooms to practise their basic skills with a teacher who is responsible for easing the pupils' learning difficulties and who, it is assumed, is able to give them a good deal of individual help and encouragement. The pupils are taught in groups, and although they often work on their own, they are frequently subjected to a highly structured environment where there is a variable degree of formal and informal assessment and a heavy emphasis on the repetition and practice of basic skills. Clark (1979) suggests that these sessions are too narrow and specific, and so different from other teaching that improvements observed by special needs teachers may not be reflected in children's regular classroom work. She concludes that there may even be some deterioration because class teachers choose to believe that they can shed some of the responsibility for the least able pupils who are receiving remedial help. For them, a special curriculum may mean no more than enhanced staffing which allows for an improved teacher–pupil ratio (often at the expense of increasing 'normal' class sizes due to the absence of flexible LEA staffing policies). Theoretically this improved pupil–teacher ratio means that more time can be devoted to each individual but it can also mean fewer specialist teachers, less advisory support, restricted access to specialist equipment and poorer quality materials. And it could also be argued that schools that add special needs departments, reading specialists, specialists in the field of 'maladjustment' and other similar personnel to an already separated 'remedial' department, do so in part to prevent the need for change by containing problems away from the mainstream classrooms.

A need for change
When HM Inspectorate visited a sample of 10 per cent of all maintained secondary schools in England in 1979, they revealed what was actually going on in many places. In their Secondary Survey (1979) they found that the majority of the teachers concerned only with remedial teaching were part-time teachers and that nearly half of them had less than five years' experience. In over half the schools visited, mainly comprehensive, HMI considered that the less and least able were spending too much time on a restricted curriculum. In schools with a higher than average intake of pupils with

learning difficulties there was often 'a combination of inadequate remedial provision in the earlier years, increasing absence, and crucial lack of help in the fourth and fifth years', so that there were 'small but disturbing numbers of pupils who could barely read at the end of the fifth year' (chapter 6, para. 2.15). Even when qualified and effective remedial help was available in the fourth and fifth years it tended, as in the earlier years, to be seen too much in isolation from the mainstream of courses and syllabuses. No examples were recorded of a 'remedial' specialist working alongside a subject specialist in the classroom, and only a few of them were involved in consultation about the syllabus or the selection of reading material, whether for a department or a main library. The 'remedial' teacher was rarely concerned with the reading difficulties of average or above-average pupils.

One of the most common failings in special needs departments is staffing them with teachers who know little (if any) more about specific teaching materials or education than those they are supposed to serve and advise. All teachers must be experts – about materials, child behaviour, strategies, techniques, management and public relations.

Barriers to change
But anyone who has worked in a secondary school will recognize the 'silent agreements' that exist, permitting certain teachers – and in some instances whole departments – to rationalize withdrawal for 'specialist help' for difficult pupils, when the 'special needs departments' (as remedial departments and special units are increasingly being renamed) feel too shaky to refuse, and may believe that pupils need to be spared from a difficult teacher. Teachers working in the same school with the same children may have completely different ideas of what education is, and far from simply being unable to agree on the solution to an educational problem, may indeed not be able to agree on whether or not a particular problem exists. And the hierarchical nature of authority in schools does not easily accommodate forums for discussion on the curriculum.

Such a lack of general discussion leads to many anomalies, for example, in the arrangements made to withdraw pupils from mainstream lessons, an issue that raises more questions than just that of labelling. From which lessons are pupils withdrawn – French? What if a school has a scheme whose content is appropriate and relevant to less able pupils? Why do some subject departments, for example English and mathematics, opt for a withdrawal system, often subsumed under the arrangement of bottom sets, and monopolize special needs staffing resources in many instances when the replacement teaching is by a non-specialist in English/mathematics? Who monitors the progress of special needs pupils – the form tutor, subject teacher/teachers, the special needs teacher/teachers or a combination of some or all? What thought is given to the amount or proportion of time that any pupil should spend in a remedial department?

Meeting the needs of all pupils
In attempting to identify and evaluate whether a school is meeting the special educational needs of its pupils, one has to examine the school's response to all the children who attend and to look at its overall organization, curriculum and teaching methods. Among the questions to ask are: is the curriculum the same for all pupils in the first three years (i.e. do all pupils take a language)? In the fourth and fifth years is there any individual timetabling, as well as options groupings? Do different subjects have the same allocated time? Does the remedial department just function as a bottom set for English and maths and, if so, are the teachers English or mathematics specialists? If there is an integrated science course in the first three years, do all pupils have the opportunity to go on to do science options in the fourth and fifth years, and if not, why not? If access to laboratories is limited, which children are excluded? Is it usually the less able, who might arguably benefit from *more* practical work, rather than less? Is the modern language course a three-year one and, if so, are children therefore excluded from the start without any prospect of participating later? Do pupils have the same teacher for the same subject each time there is a lesson? Do they have a single class base for a subject or any different English lessons held in different rooms? Answers to all these questions will indicate who is excluded from the mainstream curriculum and why, and

to what extent less able pupils' experience of school life is more chaotic than that of the more able.

Staffing
In some areas, such as Derbyshire, Nottinghamshire and Cumbria, there are moves towards 'curriculum-led' staffing policies which guarantee a base level for special educational needs, for example 10 per cent. Up to now, staffing has been provided on the basis of pupil–teacher ratios, and on the size of the school and the age of the child, there being more teachers as the pupils got older. A 'curriculum-led' model may also be a way of establishing an LEA-wide core curriculum, but at the moment, even in the areas that have introduced it (which are all areas where school rolls are comparatively small), the model is not operative in every school. The advantages of the new policy are that all pupils are more likely to participate in the full range of subjects offered and that pupil–teacher ratios may be as generous, if not more so, especially during the early years of secondary schooling. Moreover, a school that receives a 10 per cent quota of staff for special needs can deploy the teachers flexibly across the curriculum, but need not cement a separate department. (See also chapter 5 by John Sayer.)

The way forward: resource departments

A way of meeting the needs of each and every pupil in comprehensive secondary schools has been elaborated in America during the past decade and has been tried out at a school in Oxfordshire more recently (Jones 1980, 1981). Hailed by David Sabatino (1972) as a renaissance in special education, the resources approach does not regard special education as a separate system, but sees it instead as a continuum of services radiating *from* the ordinary classroom. The guiding principle is that the educational needs of all children should be met as far as possible within an ordinary school and as far as possible within an ordinary class. The resources approach emphasizes flexibility and adaptability, so that the system can be responsive and relevant to the needs of all children within the curriculum and organization of the one school, for example the mainstream class teachers co-ordinate each child's learning and the special needs teacher is the 'resource' working as part of a co-operative team. The emphasis is on the definition and solution of problems within the mainstream classroom. To enable the maximum flexibility for this model, permitting individual and small group work, preparation of resources may be required.

Setting up a resource department

The basic provision of a resource department could take the form of a room or rooms equipped according to the needs of the pupils of that school and staffed by a teacher or teachers and an ancillary helper or welfare assistant. Among the roles played by resources department staff are, first, to provide direct specialized instruction for pupils on an individual or group basis. The reasons for the withdrawal of any child to the resources base must be clearly understood by all and specific goals written down in that pupil's programme, compiled jointly by the resources staff and the class or subject teacher. The resources teacher could be concerned either with the introduction of new concepts or could reinforce concepts introduced in a subject lesson. Resources staff may also provide emotional support and encouragement for the pupil who, for example, finds it difficult to return to school after illness or prolonged treatment. Second, the resources department provides an alternative for a pupil, for example swimming at games time for a pupil with mobility problems. Third, resources staff may spend time in subject lessons, for a variety of reasons, such as helping slow learners in science lessons and reinforcing new concepts on the spot. This also provides an opportunity to monitor the level of work presented to the group as a whole and may result in resources staff preparing more appropriate material for use in specialist lessons, or enabling the subject specialist to plan for a wider ability range and thus improve the level of preparation. Working together in this way can facilitate the introduction of new teaching techniques and ways of grouping pupils. Fourth, resources staff may act as consultants on a particular pupil, and finally, they may ensure that pupils who need them receive the modified timetable and equipment that will enable them to remain with their peer group, for example, hearing aids, or ground-floor lessons for a pupil with mobility problems.

Maintaining a resources department

The resources approach is more complicated to establish than a special unit and clear guidelines are vital. As a result of monitoring a secondary school's resources department for two years, I came to a number of conclusions about the essential features of such a department. All pupils admitted to the school should be the responsibility of the whole staff, registering in ordinary classes and being retained there as far as possible. The role of the head is crucial, as innovations that cut across traditional subject boundaries are, in most secondary schools, exceptionally difficult to implement. A set of guidelines must be accepted by everyone concerned and must be open to regular review. Differences between main school and resources staff should be minimized, for example all resources staff should be responsible to the head of the school; the special schools' allowance should be eliminated and replaced by an appropriate salary structure within the school. Funding of the resources department should be built into the school's overall capitation allowance. Resource department staff should participate in the normal school duties, for example break-time supervision, and respond to main school regulations regarding absence, cover, and so on. It would appear beneficial to all concerned that resources staff should be able to offer a specialist subject in main school. Knowledge of subject curriculum planning and learning skills would appear to be essential criteria in the appointment of such staff. Specialist facilities such as medical support, physiotherapy and speech therapy should reflect the needs of the total school population. Finally, resource departments should be monitored for at least three years in order to evaluate the difficulties which arise and to increase the effectiveness of their work. Those who run such departments know all too well the depressing feelings that set in when the honeymoon period is over, usually within about 18 months. There must be a co-ordinating agent for this evaluation and it is probably not a good idea for it to be the head of the special needs department, but rather an elected committee representing both subject and pastoral teachers, as well as senior staff. This committee would serve to point up the absence, in many schools, of effective monitoring of programmes for all pupils.

Discussion: problems and advantages
Every school will have different reasons for adopting a resources approach to meeting the special educational needs of its pupils and every school will start from the different foundation of its own particular organization, existing facilities, staffing and pupils. Carterton School's resource department was set up to cater especially for children who would otherwise have gone to ESN(M) schools and who would be expected to need this kind of support right through their years at secondary school. The school was brand new, and was being built up in phases; 1978 was the first year with a fifth form, which included a wide range of pupils taking public examinations courses, as well as those with moderate learning difficulties. Many features of the school were not ideally suited to the smooth establishment of a resources department, some to do with architecture, others with teething problems over the organisation of teaching groups and with the turnover of young staff in a school still settling down.

There were problems also because of the general context of cuts in educational expenditure, which revealed the special needs department as the only growth area and so strengthened, instead of weakening, the pressure from mainstream class teachers for pupils to be withdrawn. There is also the tendency for a new department to seek an identity that is visible and consequently to attract pupils to the separate base.

Tony Booth has referred to the evaluation of the innovative Grampian team-teaching approach to meeting special needs in ordinary schools (Ferguson and Adams 1982). This study emphasizes many of the difficulties faced by resources department staff at Carterton School when they accompanied pupils into subject teachers' lessons: too little advance information on lesson content, the didactic approach adopted by teachers in classrooms, which gave no role to special needs teachers other than listening, and in many instances de-skilled them since they did not know what to do when the subject teacher was absent or delayed. Frequently the resources staff had come to accept this undemanding role (see also Jones 1981).

The advantages of resources departments in comprehensive schools are nevertheless substantial: more pupils can be kept within the mainstream of the school and the stigma attached to receiving 'special help' can be reduced; there is greater leeway for flexibility in instructional techniques, for trying alternatives, for varying approaches, and the classroom teacher is a major beneficiary because of the available feedback; the spread of expertise in turn reduces the need to identify problems. As fewer pupils with moderate problems need to be placed into self-contained classes, many pupils who have mild problems can receive assistance. This can become very critical for the pupil who is just beginning a downward spiral which in a few years would end in a special class or unit.

Not only can a resources approach meet the special needs of a wider group of pupils in ordinary schools, it also reduces the need for external specialists such as psychologists and advisers, who can therefore concentrate on the smaller number of children referred. And there is generally much greater parental and community support for resource departments than for some options existing in a typical school. A parent with a pupil who displays moderate problems is going to be much happier about a resource department than about special class or special school placement.

One of the most significant advantages of the resources approach is the possibility of changing teaching groups and the content and curriculum so that the traditional emphasis on basic skills for pupils with special needs can be shifted and their seeming all-importance for learning considerably reduced. Pupils retained in separate units frequently never get beyond basic skills because they do not use them in a range of curricular activities.

Conclusion

While it is true that the present economic climate has curtailed opportunities for more flexible teaching strategies (HMI Expenditure Report 1981) and thus poses serious difficulties for those schools that *are* attempting to create a comprehensive curriculum for all their pupils, many of the most exciting developments have actually come about because of attempts to devise appropriate curricula for children with special needs. Could this, together with the implementation of the request in Circular No. 6/81 on the school curriculum that schools, LEAs and governors make a response by 1983 towards securing a planned and coherent curriculum in schools which takes account of national and local considerations, be a more appropriate framework for progress than the disappointing Education Act 1981 (Special Needs) which gives little encouragement to those fostering innovative developments?

10

A Support Service to Primary Schools

NEVILLE HALLMARK

By far the largest number of pupils with special needs are those with learning difficulties. The traditional response to these children has been special schooling from an early age for those with severe difficulties and a pattern of crisis intervention for those whose difficulties are less serious. The limited number of places in segregated provisions and the resulting competition for places has diverted attention from providing an adequate range of help in the ordinary classroom or home.

I would argue that there has been too much emphasis on procedures that 'identify' or 'assess' pupils for these limited places and too little on examining constructive ways of supporting the efforts of classroom teachers and parents before a crisis has been reached. In this chapter I shall describe the support service set up for primary-aged children in Peterborough based at Heltwate School, a recently opened special school for pupils with learning difficulties. The views expressed are my own and do not necessarily coincide with those of the local education authority.

My experience and that of my colleagues indicates that pupils with learning problems can be maintained in the ordinary classroom longer than was thought possible. Moreover, a flexible support service can increasingly respond to children with more severe difficulties.

When considering ways and means of supporting the efforts of local primary school colleagues to meet the needs of their 'difficult to help' pupils, we soon realized that strategies such as workshop courses, short in-service courses and opening up the special school to other teachers, were by themselves quite inadequate, for there was no guarantee that they would be followed up by changes in actual classroom practices. Also, the temporary placement of a pupil in a special school or class meant that possible opportunities for helping other pupils and actively involving the class teacher were missed.

Using the model of the Portage Scheme (Weber *et al* 1975, Shearer and Shearer 1972) in which a teacher visits pre-school children, usually at home, we decided to free a teacher to visit a neighbouring school and work alongside the teacher who had identified a pupil as having difficulties. Consistent with our fundamental belief that a child should whenever possible be educated in his or her normal surroundings, we hoped, at the very least, to delay as long as possible a transfer to the special school.

Important features of our intervention in the ordinary school are, firstly, that a teacher has already perceived that a child needs extra help and so is receptive to the idea of another teaching coming into the classroom to provide support. My experience has been that most teachers are in this category and that very few remain unwilling to work co-operatively unless a crisis is reached, in which case they want the problem removed. Secondly, the visiting teacher claimed nothing more than practical experience in the use of teaching materials developed and produced at the base special school and could make available these same resources to the teacher with the pupil. All of us agreed that something tangible had to be available to the class teacher – not simply advice.

In the first instance, a young girl had been referred because of lack of educational progress, and continual and persistent demands on the teacher's time which caused the usual conflict. Our intervention, arranged through an educational psychologist, was secured on the basis of the following agreement: a visiting teacher would arrive every Wednesday for the afternoon. He would identify the work materials that would meet the curriculum needs of this girl and would then in negotiation with the class teacher identify the time of each day when they could be completed. Particular attention would be paid to providing work that could be undertaken as independently as possible, and at times of the day which had previously been the most difficult to manage. So a service emerged that combined the curriculum requirements of the pupil with practical regard to their classroom implementation. That is, notice was taken of one factor usually played down when it comes to the process of removing a pupil – the interaction of the child's demands with the level of classroom help previously available. Often it is the pupil's educational attainment or lack of it that alone confirms the apparent necessity for removal, rather than a close analysis of how alternative ways of helping the child might be attempted, a process that reinforces assumptions that the problem is wholly within the child and nothing to do with the situation in school.

The work to be achieved during the course of the next week was written down, having been agreed by the class teacher. The appropriate learning resources – workcard sheets, number games (since number work was a particular difficulty) were then provided. Success was measured by the number of pieces of work completed 'without too much extra fuss'. This could be regulated easily week by week when the two teachers met. The primary school, thus supported by learning materials together with regular 'monitoring visits', would find ways of supporting a pupil whom weeks before they had perceived as a suitable candidate for a special school. Access to appropriate curriculum materials and the writing down of weekly work objectives encouraged the classroom teacher to find suitable work for that child. A classroom assistant and even the head teacher were timetabled on occasions to help out.

The visiting teacher was able to observe and record over a period of time two main outcomes. First, that the child had gained new skills, and secondly, that the school was, by providing for her educational needs, viewing her placement quite differently. Soon there was no question of her leaving. A first intervention had taken place successfully. At this point many services would pull out since they are designed to help out in a crisis and then leave. However, the funnelling-in of learning resources for one pupil quickly led to the situation where it became clear that other similar pupils could well benefit from such an approach. As the class teacher became familiar with the imported learning materials, it was relatively easy to add a few pupils on to the list being supported. The same process was continued. Weekly work objectives were written down, based on specified curriculum needs, to be implemented by the class teacher together with whatever help she could muster. A variety of work materials were brought in which gradually formed a natural part of the classroom facilities and became readily available to those pupils who could benefit from them. A weekly visit was still regarded as important, to monitor and maintain the successful completion of work. A constructive and reinforcing relationship developed between the teachers in their respective roles. By now the visiting teacher was obliged to develop some sort of monitoring sheet to keep a record of skills gained by the pupils in order to check progress and monitor the outcomes of the intervention. What was developing was a true support and preventive service.

Clearly defined components of the system emerged as important, particularly the willingness of mainstream teachers to be involved in meeting the need of children regarded as 'difficult to help'. This appeared to us to carry a message: find ways of directly involving the teacher in identifying and then helping the pupils; circumnavigate that process at your peril. It may be helpful to summarize the stages in the process of initiating this support work to the point where perhaps several pupils could be helped by more than one teacher.

Developing a support service for children with learning difficulties in the ordinary school

1 Initial approach to referred pupil in the ordinary school. Head teachers meet and agree on weekly session by a visiting teacher.
2 Visiting teacher discusses procedure with head and class teacher. Discussion with class teacher on needs of pupil, work to be left, written down when agreed. Work done by pupil helped by class teacher.
3 Curriculum needs of child assessed. Practical consideration of how these could be met in a particular classroom. First week's work written down. Resources left.
4 Learning resources introduced gradually in response to the developing needs of the child. Any specific classroom problems noted.
5 Regular weekly visits maintained to monitor child's

progress and write new work programmes. Class teacher
thus encouraged to carry out work plans.

6 Visiting teacher devises record-keeping system, which is
open for scrutiny and which details what has taken place
on each visit.

7 Materials and teaching support clearly suitable for other
pupils, who are therefore included in the scheme as far as
possible.

8 Other mainstream teachers 'volunteer' to be helped, this
willingness being the best way of guaranteeing success.

The result of intervention was that the reasons initially given
for the child's referral for special education dissolved and the
child was successfully supported where she was. The service
spread to include more children and teachers, giving them
access to the monitoring procedure and to suitable learning
material, which became part of the fabric of the ordinary
school. The service ceased to be a crisis service and evolved into
a support service.

The pattern described for the first intervention and
subsequent initial development was in fact repeated in four
other schools, with much the same success. There were various
patterns of response to the initial intervention in the different
schools. Some schools used welfare assistants under the
auspices of teachers particularly effectively. Some decided to
appoint part-or full-time teachers specifically to help with the
visiting teacher; some used parents. What remained constant
was the weekly visit and the access to learning resources, with
written work objectives for the pupils concerned. A team of
visiting teachers soon developed at the base special school and
they decided to meet regularly each week, co-ordinated by a
senior teacher. This proved supportive to them in dealing with
problems, as well as recommending fresh procedures. After
two years' experience they all agreed about the need to do two
things. First, to concentrate wherever possible on infant age
children and secondly, somehow to devise a system which did
not exclude any child with special needs. But how do you avoid
a situation in which a teacher, now accustomed to receiving the
support, says: 'Why wasn't this child seen last year?' We did
not want a system which appeared to be an imposition,

however, and so blanket screening of children in the ordinary schools was out of the question. Instead, the visiting teachers devised a scheme whereby reception teachers, for instance, were given an opportunity to list pupils who concerned them, in order of priority, thus ensuring that the initiative came from the ordinary school about which children needed support. The visiting teacher would then collaborate on assessing the needs of these children who would be seen first.

The respective heads of the schools were to be fully informed at all times and more formally at annual review meetings. At these meetings other decisions could also be made, such as recommendation to delay transfer to junior school or for a pupil to repeat a middle infant year, often when the child had not had a full reception year. Thus all children had access to the service and potentially it was 'leak proof'. Naturally there might have to be some reordering of priorities if the numbers of children to be supported grew too large, but this was often facilitated by the teachers' ability to programme their own work, a process that in itself was healthy. However, we still considered it necessary to monitor all pupils, whoever wrote the weekly work objectives.

The process whereby a teacher had an opportunity to name pupils was repeated in September with new teachers, first, to ensure their agreement about pupils to be helped and secondly, to make doubly sure pupils were not missed. Thus it has proved possible to put into practice what the team of visiting teachers desired: a concentration of the support service in infant schools, coupled with easy access for all teachers and potentially, therefore, all pupils.

The emphasis has now shifted from the identification of pupils with difficulties to the point where sensitive help for teachers and pupils can be provided at the appropriate times by an immediately available service, maintained by the weekly visits and the necessary additional learning materials.

Before considering some wider implications, a few practical points ought to be stressed. Our experience has shown that imported learning materials have a creative effect in the schools. As mentioned before, they provide a vehicle for action by enabling more pupils to be helped in the ordinary school. Providing they are compatible with a school's own resources, teachers do not object to this 'foreign' material. On the contrary, they welcome the opportunity to use new material to gain immediate effects. A further advantage is of course that they have been tried and tested back at the base special school. Many times we have found teachers beginning to apply their own resources techniques which they learned while using the imported materials.

We have found it necessary to organize the resources for the visiting teachers, who now leave a weekly request form at the special school. This has meant some careful co-ordination at the special school and that one person has become responsible for that process and the demands it makes on the special school's own resources. Simple matters like making available good-quality card and good printing facilities, preparing workcards or games covered with protective backing material have proved a worthwhile investment. This emphasis on a developed, structured and continuous supply of coherent learning materials, in contrast to relying on *ad hoc*, on-the-spot reorganization of existing materials, needs to be stressed. And there is a further valuable development: visiting teachers and their class teacher colleagues find it very easy to agree on when pupils can be weaned off the support service.

Throughout, we have sought the regular and sustained involvement of the area psychologists. This was inevitable when we first went into the ordinary schools, but as the service developed, we felt it was important to continue the contact, which takes the form of a termly meeting at which visiting teachers describe the results of their work. It helps to legitimate the scheme, which is after all reducing the numbers of referrals to special schools. Any pupils who have needed to transfer to the special school do so only after consideration at the termly meeting and provided that their parents agree. So far, only two have transferred in four years Thus the educational psychologists are reinforcing our efforts which in turn reduces their need to become directly involved in the schools.

Our commitment to each school visited is the same (half a day a week) but the way that it is used by each school varies according to their particular circumstances. New members of staff or changes in organization because of educational cutbacks will affect the way the support service is used. The service can also respond very sensitively to the 'teacher variable'. It can recognize and take into account differences in experience, interest or ability between the various teachers without making that process uncomfortably explicit. And this factor is often the most important element in determining whether a pupil can be helped or not.

What can we conclude from the operation of this service? It is clear from our experiences in five schools that teachers appreciate it and respond positively. Certainly pupils previously regarded as 'referrable' remain in their class. Our experience is that the supported schools do not need to refer pupils 'out' except in the really exceptional cases. Furthermore, the visiting teachers often say that they are supporting pupils in the ordinary schools who have *more* difficulties than some of the pupils who come into the special school from schools that are not supported by the scheme. Without question, therefore, the system prevents segregation and promotes integration. It is also clear that teachers, by this natural process of in-school, in-service training, acquire new skills which benefit increasing numbers of children. In many instances we have observed change in curriculum organization in areas other than those directly concerning the support work.

The support service is particularly well suited to infant schools and I now feel, as somebody whose experience has been chiefly in secondary schools, that early intervention, suitably designed, is preferable in every way and ultimately more effective both educationally and economically. There has been a distinct confusion about special education for young pupils with moderate difficulties because the provision has been seen in the context of special schooling instead of appropriate help in the infants' schools themselves. People have preferred, by and large, to 'wait and see' – sometimes it is too late.

The location of the service in the ordinary school is paramount. Colleagues in special schools or other specialist bases often invite visitors into their schools or classes but frequently are unhappy about valued colleagues working elsewhere. However, in examining the provision of the future it seems clear to me that the process must start in the ordinary classroom. I would prefer this to dictate the pattern of the rest of the provision rather than the present situation, which is exactly the reverse. The whole question of where special education begins and ends would then be meaningfully blurred. Our experience shows that supported teachers will take considerable responsibility for pupils with widely varying needs, so that a clear institutional distinction is artificial and wrong.

Another feature of this support service that needs examining is the kind of working relationship that develops between visiting teacher and class teacher. Too often, class teachers or special unit teachers, for example, have to work in isolation, and would greatly benefit from sharing and solving problems with regularly visiting colleagues, provided that practical problems are discussed. Much more work needs to be done to extend our knowledge about the nature of this kind of interaction. Perhaps teachers are more open to this kind of intervention, with its constructive and reinforcing relationships, than is generally assumed.

I believe this model for providing support services has other possibilities in enabling other pupils with different kinds of needs to be helped. All pupils with special needs can be said to be characterized by the extra demands they make on the class teacher. Support to homes and schools might be similarly organized; what would differ would be the particular curricular materials or special aids and techniques. What becomes central is the organization of the support system rather than the specific need or category.

So, what will future provision look like? Will it start from the ordinary classroom and will genuine efforts be made to support class teachers to produce results that have been assumed to be out of the question? Or will we find that we end up with another form of the present system, with its inherent divisions, in which large numbers of children receive almost nothing? In looking towards future priorities, I hope I have been able to suggest some suitable starting points for constructive alternatives.

11
The Contribution of Support Services to Integration Policy

CAROLE GOODWIN

Introduction

What is the best way of organizing support for children with special needs in the ordinary school? Tony Dessent (chapter 6) argues that one way of approaching this question is to ask a second question: who takes responsibility for resolving the problems that arise in the education of children? Support services of varying kinds located outside the school have seen, traditionally, as forming a major part of the answer. Psychologists or specialist teachers are expected to resolve educational problems arising in schools through assessments and suggestions for minor adjustments in the nature of a child's education, changes in timetables or a new individual teaching programme or strategy. When a breakdown in the child's education seems inevitable an alternative, a special school, may be offered as the solution to the failure experienced by the child.

This chapter will suggest that even highly trained and well-motivated people working within external support services can be frustrated in their attempts to promote integration within ordinary schools. Based within a clinic or special school, such professionals are isolated from the mainstream of educational thought and practice. I shall examine the way the good intentions of policy-makers may fail to take account of the problems inherent in such an approach by describing three support services in Sheffield: the schools psychological service, the remedial service and the rather newer team of specialist support teachers. I shall then look at a way of organizing support within schools by a re-examination of their methods of working which emphasizes the development of a curriculum and school experience that matches the needs and interests of their pupils.

Sheffield has had a Labour-controlled council in the city for about 50 years (with the exception of one short period in 1957–58). The policy of the council has long been one of discriminating in favour of the handicapped and disadvantaged. In education, since the war, the education committee has attempted to cater for the educational needs of pupils by setting up a variety of special provision – first, schools for the blind and deaf, followed by 'open-air' schools in the more salubrious areas of the city for children defined as 'delicate'. Later, schools for the ESN(M) and ESN(S) were founded, and in the mid-seventies, separate establishments for those regarded as 'maladjusted' or for children with mild learning difficulties were opened. In all, some 2,000 children, out of a total school population of 93,000, currently attend a special school in the city, a figure above the national average. The cost per place is around £2,000 per annum – a sizeable commitment of expenditure which compares favourably with that made by other northern cities.

Around 1975 the city council also adopted, officially, a policy of integrating the handicapped into public services, and the education committee have given this policy prominence in their election manifestos since this date. They have also employed professionals who could be expected to promote this trend.

The Sheffield support services

The child guidance and schools psychological service
In 1936 the council set up a child guidance centre, which was initially under the direction of a psychiatrist. Four years later, a psychologist was appointed as principal in an attempt to make the focus more educational. The service concentrated on therapeutic work with individual children and their parents, primarily rooted in the Jungian tradition. The Underwood Report (Ministry of Education 1955) emphasized the role of the psychologists within the school system, and led to the

setting up of the educational psychology service. In Sheffield, however, this report was implemented only to a limited extent before the early seventies, as the psychologists continued to spend the majority of their week within the child guidance clinic. Both the Plowden (DES 1967) and Seebohm (DHSS 1968) reports at this time criticized psychologists for being unnecessarily isolated and remote, and at the beginning of the seventies, the newly appointed principal began to look at ways of making the service more accessible to the children in ordinary schools.

Thus an establishment of seven psychologists' posts in 1970 grew to its present complement of fourteen. Most of the psychologists are committed to implementing the council's integration policy and see their work as one means of supporting children within the ordinary schools. They have attempted to offer a preventative, as well as a remediation service, in order to avoid, as far as possible the 'waiting list phenomenon' which afflicts the work in other areas of the country. Apart from seeing individual children they have become involved in many projects that aim to prevent children' failure, such as in-service training courses and curriculum development projects.

Although the numbers of psychologists employed never reached the levels recommended in the Summerfield (DES 1968) report one psychologist to 5,000 school children, the low staffing alone is no explanation of the relative inability of the service to aid the process of integration. Their base outside schools undoubtedly did not help in making them easily accessible to the ordinary class teacher. And it was difficult for them to break away from the medical concept of their role as defining which children were in need of special help – and then recommending the most appropriate place for them to be sent. Much of the psychologist's time continues to be spent on routine assessment and placement advice. The other aspects of the work that psychologists themselves see as essential (in-service training of teachers, project and development work, counselling and therapeutic work generally) are frequently seen by teachers under stress and the employing authority as 'luxuries'. Supportive help for the class teacher is also limited by the generic role psychologists fulfil – the professional equivalent of the 'odd job man', whereas what is often sought by teachers is specialized knowledge in one area of handicap.

In an attempt to escape this dilemma many of the psychologists have helped to set up units for children with learning or behaviour problems in the ordinary school: withdrawal classes of varying sorts and other similar measures that attempt to translate features of the special school system into comprehensive schools – a step towards locational integration intended as a first step towards more meaningful social and academic integration. However, while in theory psychologists have been paying increasing attention to the systems in which they operate and which produce the problems they are attempting to resolve their influence at the level of practice has been very limited. One reason for this is that despite their comparatively high status in some areas of the education system, they do not form an integral part of the management structure of schools or LEAs and have little power to implement their views. Although many psychologists, then, envisage their role as change-agents, the reality of the situation, as witnessed by the statistical evidence given later, shows how far this ideal is from the truth.

Sheffield's remedial service

A second support service was set up in 1960 under the auspices of the child guidance service, which comprised ten teachers who worked with children defined as in need of remedial education in ten schools in the city. The children given remedial education in these schools were chosen by the school psychologists and the head of the remedial service, and were given help in a small group of six pupils on three occasions during the week. Although this was not a peripatetic service, the numbers of pupils reached in this way were very limited, and the service was criticized for being confined to only ten schools within the authority. In 1970 it was effectively disbanded as a separate entity, the remedial teachers were given to the schools in which they were already working, and the head of the service became the one advisory teacher for remedial education in the authority.

In their day, the remedial teachers were a more specialized service that looked at how children learn, and at the process of education, but they were able to reach only a tiny number of children, and did not see their role as involving the examination of how to prevent children failing in the school system.

Support teacher service in Sheffield
Following the adoption of the integration policy in 1975 the education committee decided to set up a service in 1977 which would offer help from experienced teachers in special education to class teachers who had children with special needs within their groups. This was undoubtedly seen by the Labour councillors at the time as a practical and positive step towards implementing their policy of integration, and indeed it continues to be seen in this way. The initial aims of the service were as follows (see Mullins 1982):

1 To deploy, as effectively as possible, special education expertise and teaching skills to teachers in mainstream schools who have children with special educational needs within their classes.
2 To provide (if requested to do so) information and help for the head of the mainstream school about special education provision and procedures or the services offered by another support teacher or supportive agency.
3 To notify the AEO for special education of children who might possibly be 'at risk' in the future.
4 To fulfil a preventative function, by intervening and offering prescriptive support for children with special needs.
5 To fulfil a curative function when necessary to prevent a 'failure syndrome'.
6 To facilitate the transition of children from special to mainstream schools.
7 To be available in the base special school for at least half a day per week to undertake some work within the school.
8 To liaise with other support teachers and supportive agencies.

Initially seven teachers were appointed – three based at special schools for maladjusted children, one at a school for physically handicapped, and three worked from learning difficulties centres. These appointments were in addition to, and similar to, those of peripatetic teachers based in schools for children with hearing and visual impairment within the city. Since that time, the service has mushroomed to nine teachers attached to the mild learning difficulty school, six to schools for children deemed 'maladjusted', four for the physically handicapped, and three attached to ESN(M) schools.

The support service aimed to be an accessible specialist service. Referrals came direct from the headteachers of the mainstream schools. Its creation was welcomed by teachers within the ordinary school system. In the first year of operation, Sue Mullins (1982) found that a total of 135 children were being seen by the seven teachers, and this without any publicity of the service in the city. It was also developed at a time when there was considerable criticism by some special school headteachers and teachers' organizations that the psychologists were unwilling to place children into segregated education which was producing vacancies in the special schools.

When Sue Mullins did her research in 1978–79, case loads were unevenly distributed between support teachers. Those working with learning difficulties each had between 30 and 50 children on their books. Many had already developed a waiting list for new cases and had completed few cases. With this growth, what would happen to accessibility unless the service was expanded greatly? The parallel with the dilemmas facing psychologists is striking. Had both groups succeeded in 'giving away' their expertise, advice and material to class teachers, as was initially envisaged, then a decline, rather than a dramatic increase in referrals would be the result.

The support teachers also continue to face a discrepancy between the way they see their role, and how it is seen by teachers using their service – something that has beset psychologists for years. The early research showed that 65 per cent of class teachers wanted the support teachers to be peripatetic specialist teachers, whereas none of the support teachers initially saw their role in this way. Many, however, did some direct teaching of the child, and there is still discussion in the group on this point. In addition, a few class teachers said that the support teacher acted as a 'relief teacher' to provide them with the opportunity to give individual attention to a child with emotional disorders. Perhaps this need for an extra pair of hands has increased pressure on the support teachers working in primary schools now that some part-time teachers have been cut with the declining pupil population.

Expectations of referral to this, as to any other service, tend to be high. The limited support that they can give to individual pupils seems often to produce relatively little change in performance – hardly surprising, you might think, when the minimal resources are pitted against several years of failure. But the net result of this process is that limited or no change in the children supported leads on, almost inevitably, to the call for a place in the separate special school. And this is usually supported by the support teacher herself who feels, understandably, that more time is needed, especially if small group work is unavailable in the ordinary school.

In the past two years support teachers have also helped to set up short-term units in the special schools in which they are based. Placement of a child in one of these units does not go through the normal consultative special schools procedure as the aim is to return children back to their ordinary class within one or two terms. Many support teachers help in reintroducing the children from them back into the ordinary schools. Many recognize, however, that such a short period of 'remediation' in a separate school with a separate curriculum is prone to problems of transfer of both academic content of work and social contacts and security.

How successful have the support services been?
If the efforts of both psychologists and support teachers over the last three years or so had been successful one would not only expect a declining referral rate but it may be expected that fewer special school places would be needed with the extra help available in the ordinary school system. Instead, we have seen an increase in both. In 1976–77 there were 226 placements into special schools out of 318 referrals; in 1977–78 this increased slightly to 237; 1978–79 saw 264 placements, and in 1979–80 346 children moved out of the ordinary school system. This peak, maintained in 1980, also does not include children placed in units within special schools. These figures are particularly

disturbing for the council's policy of integration when we take into account the declining school population during this period. In 1976 there were 107,019 pupils on roll in all schools in Sheffield; by 1981 the numbers had dropped to 93,251, a fall of some 13 per cent. By contrast, the numbers of children on the rolls of special schools were maintained during this period – around 2,000. Thus over this five-year period, when the policy from Sheffield education committee was to proceed with the integration of the handicapped, more children were placed into special schools, and the percentage of children within them continued to grow.

These figures are hardly surprising, however, when taken in the context of the already well-established special school sector in the city. Even if all the support services saw their role as change-agents, the inertia and vested interests they combat make it an unequal match. All of the professionals involved may well be doing other things, but they are certainly not keeping children within the ordinary schools who would otherwise be going out into the special school system.

Supporting children from within the ordinary school system

The same people who operate support services outside the ordinary schools have had considerable involvement and influence in support structures that exist within them. Such provision has been viewed as part of a continuum of services in special education which culminates in special school placement, and the same ideas of specialist responsibility and separate special education have frequently prevailed. It is hardly surprising that special classes, groups, units and withdrawal rooms mirror the segregated staffing and facilities of the special school. But there have been some attempts to change the curricula and organization of the ordinary school in order to prevent a need and desire for the referral of problems out of the school. One of the most ambitious of such attempts was described in chapter 3 for pupils with learning difficulties in Scotland.

Rather than seeking an appropriate education for the 2 per cent of pupils who may be sent to special schools, or even for the 20 per cent with special needs anticipated by the Warnock report (DES 1978) advocates of a radical shift in the conception of special education look towards what Ray Kohn (1982) calls 'the 60 per cent solution'. He argues that educational failure is endemic to our secondary school system, as 60 per cent of pupils leave school with no negotiable qualifications of any kind to show for 12 years of compulsory schooling; 67 per cent leave at the minimum leaving age, and many fourth and fifth years have already voted with their feet! Kohn argues that the aims of education are devised without reference to the students' definition of their needs. He feels that education should be seen as a lifelong process under the major control of students and parents. The onus and responsibility for learning should be placed firmly on the student. The teacher's job could become that of organizing learning material so that groups of students could decide what they want to learn and why. Implementing a lifelong self-directed voluntary education, such as Kohn advocated, would be revolutionary in Britain. Yet some of the community colleges in Leicestershire and elsewhere would see themselves as adopting an approach that goes a considerable way towards shifting the control of knowledge towards their students.

The Sutton Centre in Nottinghamshire
The 'school', catering for some 1,400 pupils aged 11 to 18, is sited alongside Sutton-in-Ashfield's new shopping precinct, and is part of a development that includes a new health centre, old people's flats, a public library, civic hall, a swimming pool and a bus station. The centre includes adult education, youth and community provision, a social services day centre, the probation service, a creche, a teachers' centre and a large number of recreational facilities. The Sutton Centre is open every evening, at weekends, and during the school holidays (Booth, Potts and Swann 1983).

The aim of the school is to provide the best of classroom management and group work current in primary education, together with the adult relationships with students prevalent in community and adult education. The teaching groups are small, and mixed ability. The students follow a common curriculum in non-streamed groups for the first five years, with an option system in the fourth and fifth year. The staff are responsible for both curriculum and pastoral matters. The teaching group is also the tutor group, with around 24 pupils. There are 12 curriculum departments, balanced in status to some extent by the point system. A remarkably informal approach is taken to social mixing between teachers and students, in the breaks taken during morning and afternoon sessions. Teaching revolves around plans for individualized learning.

No corporal punishment or detentions are used. Sanctions consist of withdrawal from a lesson, an 'on report' check with a pupil's tutor or a report system with the head. It is extremely rare for a pupil to be referred out of the centre because of difficult or violent behaviour, but it does happen. When other agencies need to become involved, they are to be found just up the corridor, and pupils can refer themselves privately.

Within the limitations imposed by the examination system, the Sutton centre has attempted to redefine school failure by defining 'success' as widely as possible. Children and their parents have a say both in the administration of the centre, and the reports that are written about them. Pupils have a voice in their tutor group, their own school council which meets weekly, and in the centre's governing body. The centre is also adapted for the physically disabled, with lifts, and ancillary helpers, small classes and so on. Yet despite the fact that physically handicapped adults are around the community centre, there are few child students who are obviously disabled (Booth, Potts and Swann 1983).

The focus, therefore, is on the education of *all* children, rather than on the needs of an identified few who come to be classed as handicapped. Some positive discrimination undoubtedly occurs, but the emphasis is on creating a flexible learning environment for all children. Children who might elsewhere be in schools for the 'maladjusted' or educationally subnormal, are catered for in the Sutton Centre because the curriculum is geared to them individually; they have stable adult relationships, and are expected to participate fully in the running of the centre.

Countesthorpe College in Leicestershire

This is a large secondary school which initially catered for children aged 11 to 18 together with a community college which offered adult education in the same building. A separate high school for children aged 11 to 14 was completed on the same campus after four years. The catchment areas of the two schools were part rural, part urban overspill. The staff of the college were appointed because of a commitment to re-examine the ways in which children can learn, and the best teaching environment for them. Leicestershire education committee had avoided building special schools for the handicapped for a considerable time and so children in the local area with all types of mental and physical handicaps became part of the school community.

In the early years of the school, children were placed in mixed-ability tutor groups, and followed a 'core' curriculum for about half of each week. The core curriculum comprised English, social studies and mathematics, which were usually taught by different subject specialists. For the remainder of the week children chose from a variety of options – some of them undoubtedly self- 'streamed' to some extent by the child's interest and ability in the chosen subject. Individualized learning methods formed the basis of the teaching, usually in small groups. In many lessons the child worked at her own pace from worksheets, and used other resources under the guidance of the teacher.

Even at this early stage in the life of the school, great emphasis was laid on the relevance of the curriculum to the needs and interests of the child. For example, the main criteria used in designing the social studies programme were to cater for the present interests of the individual pupils, and to prepare them to meet the future problems that will face them as adults. The objectives of the courses set up in social studies were as follows: to provide materials which are people-centred and involve familiar events and places rather than abstract or remote situations; to discuss historical and social conflict to help pupils choose and defend a value position; to help pupils understand the historical background to current events; and finally, to make use of pupil's feelings and experience (Griffin 1978). The role of the teacher becomes that of a facilitator, similar to the organizer of learning materials advocated by Kohn.

This reappraisal was not confined to the official curriculum; it also emphasized the importance of relationships between teachers and pupils. The staffroom served both groups at breaks, and teachers were addressed by their Christian names.

The approach to learning at Countesthorpe undoubtedly helped to support those children with special needs within the school. A separate remedial department with specialist staff also backed up the mixed-ability teaching. Three teachers, free-timetabled, worked with the first three years of pupils, as they moved up the school. One remedial teacher per year worked with the fourth- and fifth-year pupils. The main aims of this remedial department were to withdraw some children who needed extra tuition in basic subjects, to support children in the mixed-ability classes, and to provide modified materials for children with reading difficulties in subjects across the curriculum. But evidence began to accumulate that this method of working was unsatisfactory.

The modification of worksheets entailed a great deal of work for the remedial staff, frequently at short motice, and the materials produced were rarely appropriate for all pupils experiencing reading problems. Class teachers too became dissatisfied as they were using materials which they had not designed, and that were often labelled by other children within the teaching group. It became clear that the worksheet method of presentation posed several problems with many pupils who were difficult to motivate, and some change was necessary. In addition, many children as well as staff were finding difficulties with constant changes of teacher for different subjects.

Reading skills were being taught in isolation from the total curriculum, which became to be seen as unhelpful for the child's learning. Practical difficulties also arose in organizing support for pupils in ordinary classes. For example, in science, when several classes were taught in adjoining laboratories, children with reading difficulties would tend to congregate around the remedial teacher, thus forming a separate group. This in turn led the ordinary teachers to feel at a loss to develop the child's work in the absence of the remedial specialist.

After lengthy discussion it became clear that in order to

educate children with special needs effectively an alternative model of organization was necessary for all pupils in the school. Each year group of children was divided up into two teams, each having their own team of teachers. Six teachers would work with about 130 pupils for the majority of the week. Teamwork initially covered religious education, mathematics, social studies and English, but was later extended to include music, some science and craftwork. The work remained project-based and individualized, but with less emphasis on the worksheet, and more on the teacher aiding the children to plan their project and find and use resources. The children spent the other 50 per cent of their time in options with specialist staff. These groups were intended to be mixed-ability, as far as possible, although the guided choice system resulted in a degree of selection. A few slow-learning children were also encouraged to opt for withdrawal lessons in basic skills during option time or to return to their team for extra work with their tutor.

The organization that resulted from these changes was of benefit to all children, but was felt to be particularly useful in integrating those with special needs. The responsibility for both pastoral and curriculum needs of the child was placed firmly in the hands of the tutor. This was of crucial importance for those children who would normally be labelled 'behaviour problems'. Such difficulties tend to arise particularly acutely when the curriculum and teaching do not match the child's interests and capacities. The main difficulties with this reorganization tended to be those facing the team teacher, rather than the child. Because she might not feel competent in all areas of the team curriculum the subject specialists sometimes worked alongside team teachers in order to pass on their own skills.

In remedial work, the emphasis moved away from a departmental approach towards remedial work being integrated within the teams. A remedial teacher was attached to each of them, with the aim of encouraging greater informal contact between remedial and ordinary staff. Thus the needs of handicapped children were considered at the outset of the development of any new course work, and class teachers grew in confidence when handling children with special needs within their group.

The school was run along participatory lines, with all staff and children taking part in the Moot – the decision-making body of the school. The role of the head was particularly interesting in this context. He was one of the core people expected to feed in ideas to this body; he was responsible for the execution of agreed decisions, and for ensuring parental and public support for the work of the school. Another important feature was that adults were frequently learning alongside pupils, sometimes in the same classroom, as the community education and youth provision in the area were themselves integrated in the same building.

I have described in some detail the running of the whole school. The mixed-ability learning, individualized timetabling, the pastoral and curriculum responsibility taken by the tutor and the integration of adults into the learning environment all contribute to the way the school caters for those children we currently label as having special needs. In focusing on the conditions necessary for learning rather than teaching, it becomes apparent that the organization required to enable 'special needs' to be met is an essential feature of an effective learning environment for all.

Concluding remark

The two examples of the organization of community schools clearly exhibit a crucial choice facing our service. Are we satisfied with retaining the separate traditions of special and ordinary schools, but simply running them alongside one another, or are we prepared to question radically the way in which *all* children are educated in order to cater for the special needs of every single member of the school community?

12
What Difference would Integration make to the Professionals?

PATRICIA POTTS

Introduction

In this chapter I shall look at two ways in which professionals may impede integration. First, how their patterns of work and training sustain a segregated special education system, and secondly, how prevalent relationships between professionals and their clients preclude the full participation of clients in decisions about their own lives. The relative powerlessness of parents and children in their dealings with teachers and other professionals limits the extent to which children with special needs can participate in ordinary schools.

Patterns of Work

Professional investment in the present system of special education is huge. Those involved span the psychological, paramedical, educational, social, medical, legal and other professions, and the work they do may aim to be preventive, therapeutic, educational, administrative or managerial. Each profession develops a set of characterizing roles, which derive from the context and content of initial training and from the particular choice of options available, through its members, to their clients. In her article 'Professionals and ESN(M) Education', Sally Tomlinson (1981) argues that: 'All the professionals involved in special education should, despite their undoubted concern for individual children, recognise that much of what happens in special education is as much to do with their own particular vested interests as with the 'needs' of 'children' (p.277). She rightly draws attention to the existence of professional interests which may, at times, conflict with the needs of clients. But one of the main roots of present professional roles is, simply, the past; professional activities may be shaped by an inherited and unquestioned philosophy.

A widespread commitment to integration in practice as well as in theory would mean a radical change in the traditional values of our decentralized and diverse system, and would have a profound effect on the professionals. If a policy of integration were implemented, significant features of the present system would disappear or at least be drastically reduced: initial referral, transfer, formal assessment, the persuading of unwilling parents to accept segregated education for their children. The professionals that this would affect most are those who are most concerned with assessment and referral – the psychologists, school doctors, headteachers. The planning of services by local authorities would also be transformed, affecting the work of inspectorates and advisory staff, who have often made their mark in the past by proliferating segregated provisions.

Professionals spend a lot of time defining clients' needs and detecting incipient problems. Identifying children as having special educational needs is a prelude to placing them where these needs can be met, and thus depends for its validity as a professional practice in the present system upon a range of alternatives to the ordinary classroom. Educational psychologists and child psychiatrists, for example, are particularly involved with assessment and referral, with choosing the routes children will take through the system. Special education teachers, child psychotherapists and residential care workers on the other hand are predominantly concerned with teaching, therapy, treatment, care – whatever kind of continuing professional relationship is offered after referral. And these relationships become closely associated with the different institutions in which they develop. The jobs done by many professionals thus depend upon the dual system. The more a job involves decisions about moving children between the two parts of the system , or carrying out a plan of action in tailor-made seclusion, the more the duality justifies the job, and the less easy it would be to accept integration.

Isolation

As a class teacher in a special school my own isolation from local schools and from those doing a similar job was considerable. Contact with the comprehensive over the road consisted of borrowing their playground once a year for our own staff/student football match. I had little idea, therefore, of what went on in ordinary schools, what their problems were and why certain groups of children could not be included. I had no views about comprehensive education. I also had very little idea of the part that special schools played in the education system as a whole, what they were trying to do for their pupils and what effect they had on them in practice.

Later, as the remedial teacher in a child guidance clinic, I belonged to the small multi-disciplinary team of psychiatrists, the local schools psychological service group of psychologists and remedial teachers, and the scattered group of clinic-based teachers in the authority. I made frequent school visits, but it was still easy to believe that segregated provisions were therapeutic havens, that working in them made you special and that life on a comprehensive scale was to be viewed with alarm. Teaching children in twos and threes in a classroom away from school encouraged an informal style of working together, with time both to tackle acute difficulties with academic work and to develop projects on a range of subjects freed from the constraints of a more rigid curriculum. But this kind of support was short-term, 'intensive', based in a belief that remedial work at the clinic was more valuable than the efforts of the ordinary school. The focus was on the handicapping problems of children and their families rather than on constructive change within the referring schools, which were outside our sphere of influence and, indeed, interest.

Specialization

In a segregated system, most professionals specialize and only see those children who have fallen within one particular category of 'handicap'. The fashionable way to overcome the isolation of specialists is teamwork, multi-disciplinary groups providing coordinated services for the whole child. But teamwork may function to support segregation just as much as working solo. It may ratify rather than question specialization and so give the impression that all is well in the professionals' worlds, an impression that is strengthened by the following statement in DES Circular 1/83 which seems to support the notion of teamwork as doing one's own thing unchallenged, but letting the others know:

> Effective multi-professional work is not easy to achieve. It requires co-operation, collaboration and mutual support. Each professional adviser needs to be aware of the roles of his colleagues and should seek to reach agreement with them on their several roles and functions. It follows from this that his advice should reflect his own concerns, leaving others to concentrate on their particular area of expertise. (DES 1983, para. 3).

Sally Tomlinson gives us concrete examples of how much at variance are the different professionals' perspectives even on a group of children placed in a single educational category. The different accounts habitually given by headteachers, doctors or psychologists reveal that they think in different languages. No wonder teamwork is difficult: 'the development of extended "multi-professional" assessment, advocated by both the Court and the Warnock Reports, . . . assumes an unrealistic degree of communication, co-operation, and absence of professional conflicts and jealousies' (Tomlinson 1982, p.31). And it is also frequently the case that the professional with the greatest experience of a problem, for example a class teacher, is given the least weight in decision-making, for status relationships between professions are a strong influence on the dynamics of teamwork, teaching nearly always giving way to educational psychology or medicine.

Multi-professional teamwork, morever, often has very little to do with providing an optimum service for children and families, and there can be a host of reasons for maintaining this kind of contact which is only indirectly related to the concrete problems presented by clients. These problems may be insoluble by the team so that the team meeting functions to share the anxiety of its members. Or professionals may want to keep an eye on each other or, feeling it necessary to preserve a separate identity, use the forum of the team meeting to define areas of unique expertise. There are some examples, such as community paediatric teams, where physiotherapists, speech therapists and occupational therapists work together in the same room with groups of children, or child guidance clinics, where psychiatrist and psychiatric social worker may work together with families, where teamwork does refer to working with clients. However, teamwork can also mean keeping in touch with fellow professionals in conference groups to check up on work that has been done with clients individually.

A social worker who participated in a radio programme about case conferences is very much aware of the tightening constraints on his activities. He sees teamwork as essential for obtaining resources and sharing accountability in controversial cases, but he has become cynical about it as a vehicle for doing a good professional job in the interests of his clients and sees it more in terms of ritualized competition:

> All information really does have to be on the table, it does have to be minuted, it has to be sent to every involved professional in that family, and in turn they can reply and respond to anything they disagree with in the Minutes, and if the disagreement is too great to call a case conference again. Until everybody really is straight about the situation.

> A lot of my time at case conferences these days from a social worker's point of view is in to bargaining and compromise, and I go with OK a bucket full of bits and pieces and I see how few I can put on the table. It really is down to that in many cases.

> I'd like to think that perhaps more professional discretion could be given to experienced workers. The tendency these days is not to give discretion to any workers. It's to have everyone sitting round a table to make sure that everything is minuted, everybody knows exactly where one stands.

> I think certainly over the past few years there has been more an element of competition coming into case conferences, because unfortunately we've had to become more aware of scarce resources, and scarce resources obviously affect what you can offer a child. And we are

becoming more skilled at, I won't say playing a case conference, but in what we say, how we say it, and the things we are prepared to offer. And certainly when I first started in social work, oh 5, 6, 7 years ago, this didn't go on. It was a group of concerned, caring professionals sharing their views about a child, and trying to get the best for the child. Now, perhaps I do come with a slightly different angle, a different approach. Because, if I, OK if I provide a resource . . . for Mohammad in this case, it means another handicapped lad, whose parents also need relief ain't gonna get it. And it's a matter of balancing up who's the most important. What's the priority. I might as well leave this case conference to go to another one at another school, where the request is for exactly the same sort of thing. So it does unfortunately in many cases come down to scarce resources, and a fight for them. (Excerpt from Open University course E241 Radio 3: The Case Conference)

Training
Professionals usually justify their work in terms of expertise, particular combinations of specialized training and experience that become associated, literally, with different institutional territories. Like children with special needs the professionals who need them tend to follow separated routes through the system. A professional identity and expectations about a future practical role are acquired during training. Knowledge, skills and a perspective on the problems to which they will be applied constitute the expertise that justifies calling yourself a social worker, teacher, psychologist, therapist; they are the foundation of your professional rights. And the attitudes and values which develop during training may have as much significance as content and skills. In 1938 Cyril Burt wrote about the need for teachers to index-link their status with that of science:

> No layman would write to 'The Times' telling the doctor how to treat a patient suffering from bodily disease. But few laymen would hesitate to diagnose the mental state of a criminal they have never seen, to discuss the aims and

methods of educating the normal pupils, or to lay down principles for the treatment of the dull and delinquent. The teacher has never enjoyed that sacrosanct reputation of being an expert and a specialist in his own particular sphere which the doctor has always aimed for himself. . .. Nothing, I believe, would raise the professional status of the teacher so much as an attempt on the part of the teacher himself to turn his art into a science. (Quoted in Sutherland and Sharp 1980, p.191).

Professional teacher training, according to Burt's view, should, therefore, function to increase, rather than decrease, the distance between expert and client and between expert and public opinion. And this is just the effect of increasing professional specialization. Not only is specialization valued for itself alone, it also has the consequence that neither specialists nor clients find it easy to cross territorial boundaries once their place is fixed.

In *The Professionals* (Potts 1982) I sketched briefly the training patterns of some of the relevant professionals and illustrated how they came to focus on what is supposed to be unique to each profession. According to the Summerfield report (DES 1968, p.73), 'The special contribution of psychologists in education services derives from their specialised study of psychological science and its application to education and to other aspects of human development. It should be the main criterion in determining their work.'

Yet Burt himself had realized that there was no direct correspondence between psychological knowledge and the job to be done:

Educational psychology is not merely a branch of applied psychology . . . the educational investigator cannot merely carry over the conclusions of academic pyschology into the classroom. He has to work out almost every problem afresh, profiting by, but not simply relying on his previous psychological training. He has to make short cuts to practical conclusions, which for the time being leave theory or pure science far behind. (Quoted in Sutherland and Sharp 1980, p.188)

Many people, however, would suggest that the relationship between training, or the assumed knowledge base, and the job to be done is even more tenuous. In a discussion one psychologist assessed the relative merits of her training and experience:

> Eva: I trained last year as an educational psychologist and they seemed to select the people whose backgrounds they liked the look of: people with a lot of different experiences, they tend to take fewer young people now. People with a good psychology degree and a variety of relevant experience, not just the bare minimum of teaching, and they hope you're in a good enough position in your present job to get secondment.
>
> Pam: If it was all relevant experience beforehand, how does this time of training change you?
>
> Eva: It doesn't particularly. My two placements were the best part of the course, and a year's break from teaching. There was a high academic level, not particularly demanding, but with a lot of meat. You had to get through all the etiology of subnormality and autism, but it's not yet been useful to the job. . ..
>
> Pam: How far is it your previous experience or your training which give you the confidence to make decisions about which children to send and which to keep out?
>
> Eva: Mainly the experience. From working in secondary schools, I have a feel for which children will survive and which won't. On the course we rarely talked about schools, we hardly ever mentioned secondary schools. You could easily go through your training without necessarily entering a secondary school.
> (Potts and Statham 1982, 173-4)

Teachers training for work in ordinary schools are increasingly being made aware of the educational difficulties faced by children with disabilities and there is some overlap between special and mainstream teacher education. But being properly trained, professionally respectable, still implies specialization, and job-satisfaction is still assumed to depend on separate career ladders. The Warnock report made this quite clear, for among the 'skills, understanding and appreciation' that 'must be developed if the aims of the special education element' (to be included in all ·initial training courses) are to be realized are the following: 'awareness of the range of career and professional opportunities in special education, the availability of further qualifications in special education, and the fact that special education offers the teachers engaged in it an intellectual challenge of the highest order' (DES 1978, paras. 12.7/8).

The professional identity, status and continuing job security of specialist special educators advocated by the Warnock report would obviously be threatened if their training were to become less, rather than more specialized. But how far does specialized training lead to specialized work anyway? How often do people with a range of specialized qualifications actually end up doing virtually the same job? There is often a good deal of role exchange in a multi-professional team: informal counselling, practical advice and influence over placement options are a part of every team member's daily work. Indeed, this is usually welcomed in order to spread out the case load and in preference to deluging a family with professional attentions. In this way, then, expertise with clients, a style of relating to them, is assumed to be a common talent among professionals.

A more generic form of professional education, more tied to the places in which people are going to work, may be a better way of ensuring that services are responsive to genuine, and changing, needs, an aim to which most professionals give their public support. Any professional whose clients present a wide range of problems will perform an essentially generic role, despite the years of specialized training. But professionals who have been confined to a segregated special school, for example, may find the evolution towards working in an integrated setting personally very difficult as their new role may seem unfamiliar, uncharted. Seamus Hegarty and Keith Pocklington (1981a) describe the reactions of the teacher who transferred with his partially-sighted pupils to a resource base in an ordinary primary school where team-teaching was the norm:

The teacher in charge complained that the teachers with little or no specialist knowledge were deciding when he as the specialist could deliver special education: 'I don't agree that people who are non-specialists can assess whether a problem is there . . .' The perception of the main school staff was that 'the person with the know-how is not willing to pass this on . . .' Ordinary teachers were considered to be at a disadvantage in having very little specialised knowledge: 'In a way they don't think there is anything wrong with them . . . they [don't] fully understand what [partial sight] means.' (Hegarty and Pocklington 1981a, p.146)

The situation was resolved only by the retirement of the special school teacher and his replacement by a member of the ordinary school staff who had been seconded onto a specialist course on visual handicap.

Working in an integrated setting

In a system focused on the comprehensive school, ordinary schools would be enriched by the expertise transferred from special schools, utilized either in schemes of co-operative teaching in the mainstream classroom, or in resource bases where children with the range of envisaged special needs may receive particular help. Of course, in such a system these needs will inevitably change, not only as the population of the school changes, but as a curriculum is developed that can interest an increasing proportion of the pupils. The pattern of referrals to nonteaching professionals and peripatetic specialists will continually evolve so that expectations derived from a traditional training may well be confounded by the job to be done. If professionals are to be able to respond to these changing demands they must be able to change their job descriptions during their careers.

If ordinary comprehensive schools offer a continuum of provision in one place, they will become the working base for a wider range of professionals than at present, especially for visiting teachers, therapists, advisers and support staff. Relations with children, teachers, other professionals, families and local communities would also be substantially changed, as the responsibility for making educational decisions would be shifted in favour of those close to, rather than remote from, the children concerned.

Some educational psychologists have suggested positive ways in which their own profession might change: working informally with the youth service, with the ethnic minority groups; giving evidence to public enquiries and the courts, becoming involved in local pressure group politics on behalf of the families who have children with special needs. 'Community psychology should be seen as more a style of operations than a professional speciality' (Loxley 1978). Andrew Sutton (1978) argues that the present schools' psychological services be dismantled, and that educational psychologists become school, rather than local authority, based. They could then become more involved with the school's curriculum and develop a more open style of working with class teachers than is now possible. Developing a more sustained consultative role with schools rather than continuing to make occasional forays from isolated clinics or administrative offices is a vital re-orientation if an integrated system is to be strengthened.

Power relationships

The published testimony of increasing numbers of people who have had first-hand experience both of special schools and a host of professionals reveals how unsatisfactory for clients contacts with professionals can be. The insistent theme of numerous criticisms is the lack of informed power clients have to initiate, share in, or learn from the work of professionals undertaken in their name:

> None of us is at our best in our relationships with the 'helping professionals'. We meet them in the first place, after all, just because we are not at our best We are vulnerable to their power and superior expertise. We often make ourselves more vulnerable by taking off our clothes for them. We tell them all sorts of intimate details we would never normally confide to strangers. We do so because on the whole we trust that they will comfort what ails us, deliver the service they promise and let us regain

the responsibility for our own lives that we have temporarily relinquished to them. Sometimes we may be disappointed; we may get to mistrust their power and see in it an abuse of our mind, body or wallet; we may see their 'help' as a conspiracy for status; we may try to redress the balance of their power and our helplessness by taking them to court. Either way, we will usually be glad to see the back of both them and the weakness that brought us to them in the first place. (Ann Shearer 1981, p.110)

Client–professional relationships thus reflect relative positions of social power, an imbalance that is oppressively felt by many people with disabilities. Allan Sutherland presents one woman's client's-eye-view:

They reduce our ability to function independently. Because they give you the impression that they're the only ones who know what's good for you, they reduce your belief that you can solve your own problems. They therefore reduce your motivation to get things sorted out in your own life. So then they produce somebody who'll come and deal with your lack of motivation . . . (Sutherland 1981, p.129)

Nor does this perception of powerlessness only become clear to clients when they grow up. People with disabilities describe countless humiliating childhood experiences which left a lasting effect. For example, Micheline Mason endured a photography session:

I was in hospital and I was in the children's ward and they just put the screens round me and told me to take everything off. I couldn't understand and just did it. I just knew that he was taking bits, he wasn't taking me, he was taking bits of me. If they'd taken the trouble to explain what was going on, it still would not have been an okay experience, because they would have explained to me that what they were going to do was put them in a big book for medical students to stare at . . . .. And it's only one of a series of experiences, too, and they're all basically the same. Most of them are to do with men, the nurses are very different . . . (in Sutherland 1981, p.122)

And the parents of children with disabilities also suffer. Mrs Barker, the mother of a boy whose hypothyroidism was not diagnosed until he was over a year old, speaks devastatingly about her experiences of professional help:

When I had my other boy, Mike, perfectly normal, I couldn't get rid of the welfare lady . . . they kept coming round, week after week, but when I had my Kevin I never saw a soul, on my life; and that was a time when I sorely needed somebody.

For a few days they did these tests and it was proven that he was hypothyroid. But why, oh why wasn't it found out when I first took him up there when he was six weeks old . . . I shall never know. They should have gone through these tests before. I saw another specialist after he was put on thyroid tablets and he told me that owing to the fact that he didn't have the thyroid from birth he had got a bit of brain damage which could have been prevented if it had been found out earlier. And that is what made me so bitter, I don't think they take enough time and trouble. I don't know if they haven't got the time, I know they're busy, but when you're given an appointment then they should take the time and trouble, and look at everything, not palm you off with 'Come back next month, come back next month'. Because that's what I was told for nearly a year.

I got past it. I thought, if they're not going to worry, then why should I? It just used to annoy me to think that nobody came round. As I'd never had much to do with the clinic – when I went down there with my first baby, everything seemed to be so secretive. They don't tell you anything, and I hate to be treated as though I'm ignorant. This is the whole crux of the matter.

I'd have liked somebody to be visiting me, knowing how I felt, but I wouldn't have liked someone in authority. What gets me is the almoners: they've not had

any children . . . I know they get this training, but they
don't really know how you feel. They don't know how
real demented you are, indoors. You get this terrible feeling that you are absolutely . . . all . . . on . . . your . . . own.
It's you, you are the one that's important, you don't think
of anybody else, you're the only person in the world with
this worry. You go up to hospital on the day you see all
these other terrible cases, and – it's a pity to say it – it
makes you feel better just for one day, to see those others
worse off than your own, you think of those parents . . .
but then when you get back indoors you're all . . . on . . .
your own. This terrible depression comes over you. If I
could have seen someone I would have liked someone
who had the same, or nearly the same problem, the same
kind of worry. A parent. Someone you could have really
poured your heart out to and known that they could have
fully understood. When you're sort of lower class and you
get a person speaking really posh you feel . . . I don't
know how to put it . . . there's a wall. People can talk nice,
and it comes natural, you know that it isn't put on; but
then you get another person, really talking lah-di-dah and
you feel they're putting on an act. They speak as though
they know more than me . . . about my own child, or they
know better than me, about my own child. They won't
accept what I have to say. That's what people in authority
are like. (Fox 1975, pp.11–14)

How are professionals responding to these experiences of
their clients? If these descriptions are a typical sample of client–
professional relationships then you would, perhaps, expect
that some radical moves were energetically being made
towards establishing a system in which clients were treated
with respect and candour and were not excluded from any
decision making. Is this happening? Do professionals acknowledge that there is a lot that is wrong with the way they
treat clients? Do they acknowledge that partnership does not
yet exist?

Can parents be partners?
A solution to the problem of professional mystique and

unilateral power is obviously to involve clients in decision making – 'parents as partners' is the catchphrase of the moment (see for example Pugh 1981). However, there still seems to be very little of this equal partnership about. So what does the slogan mean?

There are two kinds of reply: the 'press release' and the 'internal memo'. The press release goes like this: parents make good teachers of their own children so it is a waste not to involve them; second, parents have a right to work with the professionals because they have the day-to-day responsibility for their children's care; third, sharing information and skills with parents is a more efficient way of helping children; fourth, working together increases the accessibility of professional to parents and, therefore, the familiarity that can make for greater liking and trust.

The internal memo reads: keep parents in the classroom, playroom or sitting-room and off the management committee; second, let parents support the work of the professionals rather than question it; third, as parents do not have the specialized skills and knowledge to help their children on their own, professional jobs need not be threatened; fourth, working with parents prevents them from organizing themselves too well into a separate force and can actually extend the professional role.

I do not want to argue that all press releases are insincere, nor that internal memos are necessarily more realistic, but I suggest that the contents of both should be taken seriously. I have contrasted them to jolt us into asking: does greater parent – professional co-operation result in any more parental say in the planning, staffing and managing of provisions, does greater parental involvement represent a shrinking of professional responsibility in some cases, and, lastly, does teamwork facilitate change or merely sanctify existing professional patronage? Press releases and internal memos are usually written by profesionals, not parents.

The problem with the slogan 'Parents as Partners' is that it implies that parents *are* partners, that things are all right now, and that the improvement has been easy. But making permanent changes in client – professional relationships is far more difficult. Non-specialist community workers, who have for a long time been involved in projects specifically designed to encourage the democratic participation of local families, have come to realize this. In a case study on a community project in Scotland, Jean Barr (1983) suggests that the resolution of conflicts between professionals and clients may be impossible if efforts are restricted to goodwill and small-scale co-operative schemes:

> Project leaders had to 'facilitate' the process of 'growth' on the part of individuals and groups. Thus, in their view, members of the Mothers Committee had to mature and learn how to function as a committee in order to understand the complexities of the situation facing them. This could mean that when women raised issues of concern to themselves they were deflected back to the objectives of project leaders. In this way opportunities for discussion in the women's own terms were missed. At one meeting, for example, a disagreement between the chairperson and another of the mothers over the presence of men at a forthcoming social was interpreted as an example of 'immaturity' and became a reason for mounting a course on being a committee member – thus providing a lesson in democracy. At another meeting the possibility of the centre providing day care for the children of single and working parents was raised by a single parent member of the committee. 'It would', she suggested, 'help a lot of people an awful lot'. This too was postponed to get on to the real business of the meeting and did not reappear during the evaluation period.
>
> Project leaders were in the privileged position despite their conscious democratic intent, of being able to determine the framework for the development of the project and therefore to define the terms of arguments. 'They still see us as authority – though nice', spoken with regret by an egalitarian project leader does not indicate a regrettable mistake on the part of the women in the project but an accurate perception of the real relationship involved. (Barr 1983, p.61)

And there are still professionals who explicitly reject the idea of parents as partners. For example, at a recent meeting with a divisional inspector in connection with a video project on preschool children with special needs, he was particularly concerned to ensure that I was not making an 'integrationist' film. He argued that integration was too complex an issue to be discussed by 'all and sundry'. The attitude of this LEA adviser implies that the actual consumers of services, the children and their families, have little right to be involved in any change and cannot be expected to understand the relevant issues.

Partnership in the 1981 Education Act
This sort of lack of commitment in practice to the official support for parents and children's rights warns us that partnership after 1 April 1983 may still be a mirage and makes us take a closer look at just what the Act does say. Section 9 states that parents can request an assessment whether or not their child is the subject of a statement of special educational need. However, in each case, the authority can refuse to comply if such a request 'is in their opinion unreasonable' or 'they are satisfied that an assessment would be inappropriate'. The Act gives no guarantee that parents' views will have equal weight with those of the LEA at any stage of the decision-making concerning the education of their own children.

Section 8 deals with appeals against statements of special educational need and here again, the machinery is geared in favour of the local education authority. If the parents of children who do *not* have special needs appeal against their LEA's decision about school placement then, under the 1980 Education Act, the opinion of the appeal committee is binding on the LEA. Not so with the parents of children who do have special needs. Clause 4 of Section 8 of the 1981 Education Act says that an appeal committee may either: '(a) confirm the special educational provision specified in the statement; or (b) remit the case to the local education authority for reconsideration in the light of the committee's observations.'

They are not empowered to uphold the views of the parents and make a decision independent of the LEA. Clause 5 says: 'When an appeal committee remit a case to a local education authority the authority shall consider it in the light of the committee's observations and *shall inform the appellant in writing of their decision.'* Only the Secretary of State can countermand such an LEA decision.

In an article, Freda Edis and Zena Brabazon detail the contradictions between current legislation and practice and argue that parents and children need well-organized advocates to tackle on their behalf what is, basically, an issue of civil rights. They have this to say about the new appeals procedure:

> Even at the stage of appeal, parents' rights are restricted – the parents have no right of appeal to an independent arbitration process. The appeals process is contained within the education system and parents may not challenge the composition of the local authority's and Secretary of State's appeals committee, nor, at the appeals stage, may they have their own representatives. In fact, the only time parents have the statutory right to a 'representative' is after the completion of a statement by the authority. But this representative – the 'named person' – is not an arbitrator between the parent and the authority. He or she is likely to be a local authority employee, there only to advise the parents on the child's special need, a need previously determined by the same authority's experts.
>
> To perceive the 'named person' as being the parents' advocate is patently incorrect. This part of the legislation, then, leaves the parents without objective representation. Even the most articulate are bound to be affected and those who are less articulate will find it practically impossible to disagree with the authority's decision. (Edis and Brabazon 1982, p.14)

Access to information

The kind of partnership between parents and professionals endorsed in legislation and official documents has been lopsided. The absence of any marked unease about this among LEAs or professional associations can be understood in the wider context of a belief that parents should only receive selected information from official files on their children and that professionals have the right to act as filters. The Warnock report said that parents:

should be able to see most of the factual information about their child . . . the results of professional consultations . . . would be maintained in a separate, confidential folder . . . whether or not parents are shown the actual reports on their children must be a matter for the judgment of the professional concerned . . . The over-riding consideration should always be whether or not it is in the child's best interests that the parents see the reports on him. (DES 1978, para. 16.12)

DES Circular 1/83 does go further than any previous document in granting parents access to information about the assessment of their children and has been hailed as a breakthrough by some pressure groups (Advisory Centre for Education 1983). Parents of the small group of children (approximately 2%) who will be subject to formal procedures of assessment (statements) will have a right to see all the advice from various professionals on which the assessment is based and there is an exhortation to take their views into account: 'In looking at the child as a whole person, the involvement of the child's parent is essential. Assessments should be seen as a partnership between teachers, other professionals, and parents, in a joint endeavour to discover and understand the nature of the difficulties and needs of individual children. Close relations should be established and maintained with parents and can only be helped by frankness and openness on all sides.' (DES 1983 para.6) However, 'the ultimate responsibility for assessing the child's special needs rests with the LEA', and it is up to the LEA 'to decide on the weight to be given to different kinds of advice', including the parents' (DES 1983 para.39). Nor is there any suggestion that school records should be open to children, nor that assessment procedures should be revealed to parents if used on non-statemented children. The official participation of parents finishes once the statement has been agreed. (For an excellent exposition and interpretation of the 1981 act and parental rights see Newell/ACE, 1983).

Keeping files secret from parents on the ground that their contents may be painful to them only shows how far professionals have removed themselves from the very issues that have to be confronted. Records are frequently speculative, vague or irresponsibly brief. And they can also be casually damning. Warnock claims that parental access would mean that reports could become less detailed, but it might be sobering for many professionals to examine exactly what the detail presently consists of. And it is often the case that information on confidential files is not much used even by the professionals; it is by no means automatic that teachers, for example, get to see reports written by psychologists on children in their classes:

> It has surely got out of hand when a letter from a child guidance clinic containing travel instructions is headed 'confidential' because the printed stationery of the clinic automatically bears that heading; or when the psychologist's report with its printed 'confidential' heading goes straight from the headmaster's desk into the filing cabinet and any useful contents it might have had for class or subject teachers is never exploited. (Fitzherbert 1977, p.101)

As long as the professionals are regarded as the experts and the education authorities as the sole guardians of control over resources, then arguments for open records will not gain much official ground. But in a genuinely comprehensive community-based system of education, which values a range of sources of information and insists that people are involved in making decisions that affect their own lives, such accessibility would naturally follow: parents and older pupils would have automatic access to relevant files and would have control over who else is allowed to see them; their dissenting comments would be included alongside the professionals' statements, and they would have their rights clearly set out for them in writing.

What will happen?
A national persuasion that children should be educated at their local ordinary school would thus entail a rejection of the traditional reverence for specialization, a transformation of our competitive school system and a thorough overhaul of the existing professional services that support it.

The stumbling block to the changes necessary for the inauguration of an integrated system is that they threaten values much dearer to many British hearts than their state education system. Encouraging professionals to abandon ideals of service and autonomy in favour of a consultancy which is explicitly accountable to clients and which rates commitment and experience above certificated specialization, might be to urge an unpalatable change in their conditions of hire and source of work.

After the 1981 Education Act has been implemented in April 1983, therefore, and children are no longer assigned to categories of handicap but placed along a continuum of special educational need, what will happen to the professionals? Sally Tomlinson is convinced that their numbers will continue to grow:

> The new processes of referral and assessment for an expanded special education system will increase the number and type of professionals whose judgments are used to separate special children from ordinary children in schools. The adoption of the care of 'special educational needs' as a rationale for this separation, and the abolition of statutory categories of handicap are likely to give more, not less, power to professional people. While the assessment processes beyond Stage 3 will increase the numbers of psychological and medical personnel plus other professionals such as social workers, and speech therapists, it is educationalists, particularly heads and teachers in normal education, who will have increased powers to decide that larger numbers of children have special needs, and special educators who will have expanded professional interests in making provision for these children, in special units and classes as well as separate schools. (Tomlinson 1981, p.276)

When discussing LEA views on integration or their plans for implementing the 1981 Act, advisers for special education not surprisingly, perhaps, seem to focus on the question of the efficient use of resources, which in section 2, clause 3 of the Act can be used as an argument against integrating children with special needs into ordinary schools. One adviser I heard recently believes that there are children for whom the ordinary school would be a deprivation and that no substantial moves can be undertaken until the ordinary schools are fit to receive new pupils. His message was, in fact, that integration is extremely difficult, and, offering no positive suggestions either for the transfer of expertise from special to ordinary schools, or for the successful preparation of mainstream, it was quite clear that he had no plans for integration and certainly was not encouraging schemes to get off the ground.

There *are* signs of progress, however, and these are coming particularly from parents of children with special educational needs and from people with disabilities, whose voices are strengthening both in protests against professionals and in clearly articulated demands for reform. In *Disabled we Stand* Allan Sutherland (1981) described how a support group of people with a wide range of disabilities developed an active political role:

> We have used the confidence and solidarity we have drawn from the group to start working together politically: making contact with other people with disabilities in order to share support and information with each other; initiating and providing support for campaigns which fit in with our views on disability; publicising those views by such means as providing speakers, writing, giving interviews to journalists and making careful use of television and radio . . . we formalised our political activity by setting up a group entitled the Liberation Network of People with Disabilities. What is important . . . is that the able bodied be prepared to recognise our expertise, on the simplest level, we know best what our individual needs are; and when it comes to working for change, we are the people who know best what our oppression consists of, because it is we who experience it. The extent to which we can work with the able bodied is entirely dependent on how far that recognition is present. We have all had quite enough of able bodied 'helpers' doing things for us (whether it be pushing a wheelchair or trying to influence legislation and

social attitudes) in a way that reduces us to unnecessary dependence and fails to do those things in the way we want them done. But when the able bodied recognise our right to control our lives and determine our future for ourselves, they can be valuable allies. (Sutherland 1981, p.113)

In the run-up to the implementation of the 1981 Act, parents' groups are publicizing their views about co-operation with professionals and outlining the sort of equal partnership they believe to be essential. Family Focus, an active group of parents of mentally and physically handicapped children in Coventry, has produced a discussion paper on 'Parental involvement in the assessment of children with special needs', in which mutual respect and information-sharing are major themes. One of their fundamental demands is that of access to professional reports and deliberations about their own children:

We feel that professionals should give parents detailed written reports of their assessment of any child. Just as it has come to be regarded as good practice for professionals to share such information with each other, so should they expect to have to share it with parents . . . . It is common practice for professionals involved in assessment to meet together to discuss their findings and to advise each other on the implications of their assessment for decisions which have to be made. We would like to see a situation in which parents could attend and play an active and significant role in these case conferences . . . There is crucial information about our children's abilities, disabilities and special needs which can only become available to professionals if they involve parents fully in an assessment procedure . . . . Just as we recognise how reliant we are upon the knowledge and skills of professionals, we feel that professionals too, must seek to develop forms of practice which recognise the crucial nature of the knowledge and skills which parents have. (*Family Focus* 1982, *WHERE,* no.183)

Finally, these parents acknowledge that the partnership should be three-way wherever possible: 'Professionals and parents should try to see the child as part of that partnership too, particularly where an older child is concerned. To that end, we have to recognise that our views are not always congruent with their views about their own needs.'

Meeting the special educational needs of children and young people is not therefore just a question of providing improved welfare services and more specialist experts, but has to do with a fundamental acceptance of all children's and adults' rights both to education and to participation in their community. This cannot be realized in a system that continues to deprive the consumers of services of their share in the planning and control of these services and fails to acknowledge that professional accountability has to include being accessible to critical clients who, although without the power to distribute resources and salaries, are nevertheless members of the society from which these resources are drawn.

13
Summary and Prospect

PATRICIA POTTS

How should integration proceed?

There are several themes running through the chapters of this book: integration needs a context of comprehensive schooling, community support and influence, shared responsibility for all children, clear policy statements, reallocation of resources. Integrating special education thus entails profound changes throughout the education system. It is a process not solely concerned with transferring children, resources and professional expertise from specialized to more community-based settings, but also with the whole range of factors that impede transfer. This view is reflected in the number of chapters which have discussed the necessary reorganization of mainstream schools, support services, local authority administration and procedures for national policy-making. The absence of a genuinely comprehensive ordinary school system maintains the pressure to refer children with difficulties out to separated provisions: putting a stop to segregation is an inescapable part of the process of integration.

Facilitating integration involves a reassessment of the dominant values of selection, competition, specialization, and the reorganization of many features of daily school life. Relevant innovations described by contributors to this book have included: co-operative teaching, mixed-ability groupings, resource bases, curriculum developments, bringing support services into the ordinary schools, and the merging of explicit responsibility for children with and without special needs among headteachers and local authority personnel.

Tony Booth in chapter 3 illustrated how the determination

to avoid alienating and denigrating less able pupils has led to the development of co-operative teaching between remedial and class teachers or subject specialists in the Grampian region of Scotland; a concrete move which derives from an active policy commitment and the consequent allocation of funds for staffing. Neville Hallmark's scheme based at Heltwate Special School (chapter 10) also depends upon co-operative work between teachers, both inside and outside the classroom. Team teaching, which aims to prevent the rejection of pupils from ordinary groups, thus making these ordinary groups more heterogeneous, shows that mixed-ability teaching groups are another implication of moves towards comprehensive education. Children in selected groupings for less able pupils usually find that their curricular diet is severely restricted or quite different from that served to their more able peers.

Carole Goodwin in chapter 11 has described how mixed-ability teaching groups in small, stable groups can ensure that all pupils have access to the whole curriculum. Co-operative teaching enables this to take place on a variety of levels within one overall group. Jean Garnett's peripatetic remedial teachers in Coventry (chapter 8) work with class teachers with this specific aim in mind: to support pupils as full participants in their ordinary groups rather than take them off for specialized treatment. Keeping pupils together in unselected groups and bringing support services into the classroom imply, in turn, new ways of defining and designing the curriculum itself: what is to count as legitimate content, what is to be the range of activities undertaken by the pupils, what are the variety of acceptable teaching styles?

If children are not creating a flow from mainstream education when they experience difficulties which prevent traditional academic and social success, then increasing flexibility within ordinary schools must extend to provision for those whose problems may not be erased by opening up the classroom and the curriculum, Elizabeth Jones has described in chapter 9 how resource bases within ordinary schools can form an important link in meeting the range of special needs that there may be in a school's community. They are an essential progression away from special units catering for designated groups of pupils. Many so-called 'integration schemes' are perfectly compatible with selection and specialization because they use separate premises and house a supposedly homogeneous group of children. Resource bases, on the other hand, increase the range of provision under one roof, but by way of providing a despecialized centre for a variety of specialized services.

Team teaching, mixed-ability teaching and the introduction of resource bases all have implications for staffing ratios and the rationales used when they are calculated. John Sayer argues in chapter 5 that staff shortages are the major stumbling block to comprehensivization because they force schools to continue with large classes and unsupported teachers, making segregation for some inevitable because alternatives cannot be established in the ordinary school. He questions the whole basis of educating children in class groups and is concerned to develop an awareness of the value of those activities – creative, therapeutic, uncompetitive – that takes place outside the monolithic classroom, but which are the first to go when teaching and ancillary staffs are reduced.

If it is the proper job of an ordinary school to provide services for a wider population of pupils than is now included, then headteachers and LEA officials must accept responsibility for this wider population without distinctions. Tony Dessent argues in chapter 6 that the reluctance to accept this responsibility perpetuates both the separation of different sectors of the education system and what is seen as their competition for resources when attempts are made to bridge the gap. Integration is needed at every level of the system, among professional hierarchies just as much as in classrooms and staffrooms, and this is one of the main concerns of Neville Jones (chapter 4) in his discussion of ways of integrating local education authority administration.

If the contributors to this book are all committed to moving the education system in the direction of comprehensivization and therefore also to meeting special needs in mainstream schools, there are nevertheless some important issues upon which they are not unanimous. For example, they disagree about the location of support services and about the value of using the techniques of behaviour modification. Jean Garnett (chapter 8) and Neville Hallmark (chapter 10) describe schemes that are designed to prevent referrals to segregated provisions and do involve teachers with experience of children with learning difficulties going into mainstream classrooms. Nevertheless, these services remain based outside the ordinary school, employing staff whose primary responsibility does not lie within the mainstream provision and thus perpetuating the idea of separate, specialist expertise.

Specialist support services which explicitly set out on a programme of prevention, or individual schemes devised to meet special needs in an ordinary setting, may have an effect which is directly opposite to their stated aim of promoting integration. Carole Goodwin (chapter 11) illustrates how the proportion of pupils in segregated provisions in Sheffield has increased, despite the creation of a support service designed to keep referrals down. Educational psychologists and peripatetic remedial teachers also found their efforts backfiring on them as their specialized base outside the ordinary school and the lack of a coherent LEA-wide policy meant that hard-pressed teachers in ordinary schools heaped them with referrals, which were dealt with in a piecemeal fashion, using but not transforming existing provisions.

There is disagreement too about the pace and extent of integration. Colin Low in chapter 2 argues for what he calls a 'moderate' position, which involves a centralization of provision for blind students within designated schools. He argues for the retention of some residential special schooling for the multiply handicapped, though others might argue for their inclusion in centralized resources in ordinary schools with other profoundly handicapped children. His description of provision is closest to the unit model as opposed to the flexible resource base advocated by Elizabeth Jones (chapter 9) or Jean Garnett (chapter 8). When services for children with disabilities are delivered into the normal classroom in a team-teaching situation perhaps the need for specialists uniquely related to particular disabilities will begin to be eroded.

Tony Dessent (chapter 6) has suggested that children without visible handicaps pose the greatest challenge for integration because it is harder to see their difficulties either as someone else's responsibility or as due to a disability. Tony Booth (chapter 1) suggested that it is disaffected pupils who are the one group whose very presence in the school demands more than a token reorganization. It is clear from the experience of authors of other chapters that what one area of the country regards as difficult or impossible another area of the country may be attempting with some success. John Sayer (chapter 5), Jean Garnett (chapter 8), Elizabeth Jones (chapter 9) and Neville Hallmark (chapter 10) all describe ways in which children with moderate and 'invisible' learning difficulties can be retained successfully within ordinary schools.

Jean Garnett and Neville Hallmark are also the protagonists of behavioural, objectives-setting approaches to the teaching of children with special needs In this case, Will Swann (chapter 7) is their main critic. Arguments in favour of a behaviourist approach include the following: behaviour modification techniques provide a concrete, realistic framework for teaching, and the setting of concrete objectives in a series of small steps offers more chance of success for the children and a more accurate assessment of their capabilities than generalized normative assessments that make insidious comparisons; behaviour modification does not have the treatment connotations of a medical model of learning difficulties, giving as much weight to environmental factors as to the personal characteristics of an individual child; the language of reinforcement and extinction may be another way to understand a child's problems and therefore boost the confidence and optimism of child, parent and teacher; behavioural techniques can also be used, as are those described in this book, as preventive measures, ways of identifying incipient difficulties, or relatively non-verbal methods of early intervention which may avert more serious difficulties later.

Jean Garnett and Neville Hallmark are particularly concerned with children with mild and moderate learning difficulties and Will Swann illustrates his point with reference to children whose problems are far more severe. However his criticisms are of the behavioural approach as a whole: behaviour modification and the setting of behavioural objectives are a structure for doing something, by themselves they are content and context free. Yet lists of objectives are often described as a 'curriculum'. From the pupils' point of view, the series of small steps outlined in a behaviourally structured programme of work are usually abstract and meaningless and serve only to widen the gap between struggling pupil and technocrat teacher. In this way, behaviour modifications may be a new professional mystification, a new role for psychologists who have abandoned psychometric testing. It is also a new way for professionals to control and patronize children and parents, not only because the strategies they use seem to require a lot of jargon and paperwork, but because the value-free nature of behavioural techniques is a myth. The very setting of objectives assumes that there is a good which is aimed at.

If you look at the stack of Portage cards (Shearer and Shearer 1972), you will see that there is a section on etiquette and manners which may be totally at odds with the lifestyles of the families involved. Parents may feel that, again, decisions, regarding their children have been taken out of their hands. On the one hand, therefore, there is the 'training' image of behaviour modification, which can be seen as just as insulting as regarding some children as ineducable; on the other hand, there is a subtle set of professional values which are individually wrapped for each child. Will Swann acknowledges that behavioural techniques with severely disturbed children who have very little language may well be of enormous help both to them and their families when it comes to toilet-training, self-inflicted violence or vandalism, but there remains the huge problem of generalization to other contexts and over time.

Integrating education, health and social services

This book has focused on the development of coherent policies for comprehensive education and practices which facilitate the retention of children within their local community. An integrated education system, however, cannot be achieved in isolation from other statutory services and it is not enough merely to advocate increased liaison and consultation in individual cases. Support from all services has to be co-ordinated on the basis of a common policy area, as Tony Booth argues in chapter 3, for otherwise developments within any one service will be piecemeal and fragile. If the health and social services in an area are making extensive use of segregated institutional placement, for example, then schemes such as linking health care to community education centres, or for twinning ordinary and special schools as one way of setting the process of integration in motion, may be invalidated. Accepting that all children have a right to receive services that meet their needs without removing them from their home community is a part of accepting that this principle holds good for everybody. Moves towards integration must involve adults as well as children and, therefore, the full range of services that people might need during their lives.

The view of inter-service co-operation contained in the DES circular 1/83 and the 1981 Education Act, however, does not include this dimension of explicit policy-making based on a shared social philosophy. Collaboration between services is envisaged for assessments of the special education needs of individual children. The picture which emerges is of a series of one-off advice-sharings to co-ordinate a range of perspectives on a particular child, supplied by professionals whose fields of work are essentially separate.

Taking care to collect as many professional reports as possible during a child's assessment, however, may have the result of confirming segregation rather than that of guaranteeing the maximum integration possible:

> The new processes of referral and assessment will increase the numbers and types of professionals whose judgments are used in the assessment processes . . .. Developing special education in integrated settings will demand more, not less, professional expertise, and the increased use of professional mystiques may be used to legitimate the processes that segregate normal from special. (Tomlinson 1982, p.181)

Sally Tomlinson's fears were echoed by a group of doctors who met last year to discuss the integration of statutory services. They argued that assessment often resulted in the undesirable labelling of children and that a good deal of professional time was spent on assessment as an end in itself and then used to remove children from their communities. A commitment to the elaborate machinery of assessment makes changes in provision extremely difficult, especially when the numbers of professionals involved are large. To make sense of assessment, it has to be done in the light of possible options for subsequent action, and if there are only two available – mainstream classroom or special school – then what is the point?

Constraints on developing closer working links between health, education and social services are historical and administrative. One of the most frustrating is the way in which the services are organized into geographical areas that do not coincide. In Birmingham, for example, there are five health districts which do not correspond to the divisions of the local education authority nor to the social services administrative areas, and which do not themselves contain an equal number of school clinics.

The way resources are distributed and the structure of planning and consultative committees also vary from service to service. There is a greater degree of centralization in the use of resources in the health service, based on economic considerations which are now being challenged within the education service. At a discussion group convened to examine these issues a hospital-based paediatrician adhered to the traditional view on the grounds of practicality, but several counter-arguments were put. For example, if children were not moved around between segregated provisions then other sorts of work would be reduced, making a reallocation possible without involving vast new sums of money. If the pattern of education was different, the work that the health professionals would be required to do would also be different and consultants who went to see children in ordinary schools might have more time for such visits.

Another example demonstrates that there are values which cut across economic efficiency arguments and which may be more powerful:

> It might be terribly convenient to have old people in old people's homes, have them all shift into old peoples homes, so you can deliver services to them in a very concentrated and convenient way, but actually the decision about whether or not they're in old people's homes isn't, can't be made on that basis. (Discussion group, January 25 1982)

The internal politics of the professions involved constitute a third kind of barrier to the integration of the statutory services. In an article on the school health services and their role in the integration of children with physical impairments into ordinary schools, Katrin Fitzherbert echoes the criticisms of educational professionals: 'At the root of current problems in school health is an unresolved conflict of interest between, on the one side, the health needs of children, and on the other, a satisfactory career structure for doctors' (Fitzherbert 1982, p.101).

Focusing on the needs of children in a mainstream setting would, she argues, be unacceptable to the BMA because it would upset the present balance of medical power:

> The school doctors (or CMO's) would dearly love to have accepted Court's challenge to acquire the medical expertise called for by health needs of today's children. However, in the BMA they are traditionally represented by the 'community medicine' committee (other special-isms in this faction include public health, community geriatrics, family planning). If CMO's defected to join the GPs or the hospital doctors' (paediatricians) faction, then the strength of the community medicine faction would be seriously weakened. Thus, medical politics brought the school doctors' aspirations to nought. (Fitzherbert 1982, p.101)

This resistance to change on the part of the most powerful profession brings us to a fourth barrier to integration, that of the creation of new jobs. Katrin Fitzherbert describes how the proposals contained in the Court Report (DHSS 1976) for the appointment of general practitioner paediatricians (GPPs) have foundered. Where would this new breed of community worker fit in? Wouldn't they get in the way of the family GPs? The Court Report saw the new GPP as a doctor who would work with the chronic problems of disability and stress: 'a shift of emphasis from curing to caring and prevention' (Fitzherbert 1982, p.101), and who would be active in local schools.

Another recent example of hostility towards a new sort of professional was the reaction against the Jay Report's (DHSS

1979) proposals for a care worker for community-based long and short stay provisions for mentally handicapped children. The plan was to train people, not as nurses, but as community care workers, with a joint grounding in social and health work. One of the doctors at the 1982 discussion group saw this response in the context of the breaking down of training patterns, a far more serious issue than that of a superficial willingness to liaise from day to day. However, as she argued: 'A separate initial training really roots one in such a way that it really is difficult to work together later on.' Moreover, the nursing unions, who were the groups most threatened in this case, would have to face the loss of jobs if the proposals went ahead.

Finally, a social worker in a rural area is keenly aware that the pressure to segregate is not just a feature of the education system: 'An integrated education system alone is not enough. Where children live, sleep, eat and play is, to me, as important to that child's future place in our society . . .. Lifestyle and education go hand in hand' (Paula Toyne 1981, p.1).

Working in a rural area, she is conscious of the ways in which children are frequently removed from their family home, local school *and* community and placed in distant residential provisions. Efforts to reverse this trend have resulted in a philosophy of care in the community which implies a policy of integration for all services because they cannot work in isolation. Care in the community also implies a range of options so that children whose own families find it hard to cope can still be members of their home communities. The kind of new professional to value and support may be a substitute parent, not a high-ranking administrative assessor or graduate paediatrician.

The obstacles in the way of integrating the education, health and social services are thus varied and hardy. However, each of them has implications for the shape, size and functioning of a service that was integrated, for example: flexible and evolving professional roles; community-based offices which are easily accessible to local people; specialist support services organized on a community basis and delivered to non-specialized places like ordinary schools rather than locked up in particular institutions; more attention to the less prestigious workers such as school nurses, welfare assistants, substitute parents; new types of provision, such as school consortia with their own health centres.

What will happen?

There are three possible views of the 1981 Education Act. You can see it as a landmark in the progressive development of education for children with special needs; you can see it as a subtle exercise in the tighter control of undesirable groups of children and their families in a shrinking and increasingly competitive education system; or, lastly, you can see it as largely irrelevant, a formal document empty of content, which leaves LEAs free to carry on as before or to make changes, as they wish. Certainly, as a policy statement, the Act bears little resemblance to policy as defined by Tony Booth in chapter 3, being uncommitted to any specified direction of change or any clear end-view of the kind of education system towards which we should be working. John Sayer (chapter 5) is sceptical about the connection between legislation and the eductional needs of children; the contributors to this book do not see the 1981 Act as a support for their efforts to make schools more comprehensive.

Rolf Hermelin, on the other hand, writing as the director of parliamentary affairs for MENCAP and president of the National Council for Special Education, says: 'If the new Act has done nothing else it has firmly established the legal, administrative and philosophical base on which a healthy future for special education can be built, at least to the end of this century' (Hermelin 1981, p.7).

But the 'healthy future' Rolf Hermelin envisages includes a segregated special school sector and he makes no bones about his attitude towards comprehensive schools.

It must also be borne in mind that it is now universally accepted (with one or two exceptions raised by those who advocate the wholesale shift from special to ordinary school, with no regard to the severity of handicap or emotional disorder many of the children have) that special schools will not only remain but will play a more important role than they did hitherto. These schools, as the Warnock Report recommended, should become resource centres in the sense that teachers who are teaching children with different handicaps, perhaps in ordinary schools, will be able to get expert advice there. Teachers in special education today will have to play a vital part in this development to becoming the core element of these new 'special teachers' centres'. (Hermelin 1981, p.7)

So, what is good about the Act, which is supposed to encourage the integration of children with special educational needs and to recognize their right to be in ordinary schools, is that it is going to make it possible to strengthen segregation. This is the trouble with praising the Act for being a piece of enabling legislation – it means that contradictory developments are both sanctioned (see chapter 3).

In predicting what will happen after the implementation of the Act in April 1983, we have to consider not only the problems faced by particular children and particular LEAs, or the professional needs of those currently working in the special education section, but also the wider significance of the designation of a child as having special educational needs. It is this omission which the fiercest critics attack.

Will the over-representation of black working-class boys, for example, continue now that specific categories like 'maladjusted' and 'educationally subnormal' have been abolished? Will arguments about cultural disadvantage help to determine who has special needs and so perpetuate the old forms of patronage, even if special education is increasingly to be found in the ordinary school? Sally Tomlinson argues that this will be the case, and for good reasons:

Special education within normal schools may develop as a powerful legitimator for the increasing unemployment of a larger number of people. To have received a special education – with its historic stigmatised connotations – even a non-recorded special education in an integrated setting, will be regarded unfavourably by potential employers. (Tomlinson 1982, p.177)

Society, or rather the dominant groups in society, will still need to segregate considerable numbers of children. This will be done in the guise of what Sally Tomlinson describes as 'benevolent humanitarianism', backed up by an 'increased use of professional judgments'. After reading Rolf Hermelin's article her fears seem to be justified. She also foresees the crystallization of 'a new tripartite system of education' in Britain: independent, comprehensive and special, which will function 'to preserve the social, economic and cultural status quo.'

Geoffrey Bookbinder, an educational psychologist, points out that the benevolent camouflage 'is a way of alleviating the problems of the school rather than those of the child' and criticizes both the Warnock Report and the 1981 Act for ignoring the problems of schools and consequently for not making any recommendations for constructive change: 'If the schools are failing to provide adequately for the majority of those who attend them, how can they be expected to meet the educational needs of the least able and the handicapped who will require additional resources and staff for which finance is unavailable?' (Bookbinder 1982, p.40)

However, while this argument fits neatly alongside those of Rolf Hermelin for boosting the special school sector, Geoffrey Bookbinder does not leave the issue there. He argues that there are advantages and disadvantages to be found in both ordinary and special schools for children with special educational needs and that neither setting is at the moment equipped to meet them: 'The concept of special educational need with its accompanying assumption that such needs can be adequately met in our present education system is thoroughly unrealistic and is likely to lead us astray. A more realistic concept, in my view, is that of least disadvantage' (p.41).

Geoffrey Bookbinder believes that the Act leaves schools and professionals ample room for segregating children on educational grounds, but he also believes that, even if it is true that a child's educational needs might be better provided for in a special school, there may still be other, more important factors to weigh up, which indicate that on balance the ordinary setting would be more beneficial: 'The fact that some of the child's needs are not met in one school does not entitle us to transfer him to another in which more important social and emotional needs, that go beyond what happens in school, may be frustrated' (p.5).

He argues that we should set the 'narrow world' of school into the 'real world' of the child and his or her family and judge the pros and cons of integration from this wider perspective. Most important of all is to discover which sorts of needs matter most to the families and to decide on educational placement only in the light of their views. This 'realism' is not part of official rhetoric and thus the 1981 Act perpetuates a hollow process: 'We will go on pretending that we can identify and provide for special educational needs. Children will continue to be artificially assessed by people they have never seen before and emphasis will continue to be placed on the child's defects rather than on the limitations of the system to cope with them' (p.6).

It is not just those who are particularly concerned with the special needs of children who share this pessimism. Richard Pring, current President of the Confederation for the Advancement of State Education (CASE) also envisages a retrogressive hardening of the divisions between the private and state-maintained sectors of the education system, between the academically able and the less able, between the rich and the poor:

> The maintained sector of education is publicly criticised by the very Ministers of State who are given responsibility for it . . . Essential resources are being taken away at the very time when subsidies to the private sector are being increased. The one area of rapid expansion – namely, the pre-vocational 16+ training programme – is being financed and controlled, not by the education services . . . but by a quango within the Department of Employment. The closure of the Schools Council reflects a distrust in the professional capacity of the teaching body to sort out curriculum problems. (Pring 1983, p.55)

To Richard Pring, the policies of the present government represent 'a return to an elementary school tradition within the non-privatised sector' in which those who run the state schools are a privileged group who do not use them for their own children and in which the curriculum is restricted to the 'socially useful and the practical but discouraged critical reflection and acquaintance with wider cultural values'. Cuts in resources, therefore, are not just the result of being short of cash but have a significance which is 'more dangerous', reflecting 'an important shift in educational thinking' which has meant the withdrawal of support from the maintained sector and 'the determined pursuit of privatisation'.

LEA trends

Listening to what local education authority officers say about their plans for implementing the 1981 Education Act, it is hard not to believe that the pessimists are right, for the kind of rhetoric they use is often quite obviously camouflage. One officer said recently, when asked for a brief policy statement, that his authority was 'fully committed to implementing the 1981 Act, to identifying good practice and to improving the lot of children with special needs'. Which, of course, tells you nothing about their policy, except, perhaps, that it does not exist.

Within the rhetoric of integration what is actually happening are responses to economic and administrative pressures, or to the initiatives of single officers, headteachers or other professionals, but very rarely any active lead in promoting policy reform. Looking through the case studies in *Integration in Action* (Hegarty and Pocklington 1982), this appears as a recurrent pattern. Describing a scheme for the individual integration of children with physical impairments, the authors note:

This integration programme developed in a relatively piecemeal way through individual initiative and parental pressure . . . .. It became established as the primary educational route for physically handicapped pupils in much of the authority in a de facto way rather than as a result of a formal LEA policy decision. Indeed, the LEA maintained a background role for many years, acting in response to representations made or pressures applied. (p.93)

One of the conditions laid down in the 1981 Act to be satisfied before the integration of a child with special needs can take place is that such an arrangement should be in line with the 'efficient' use of resources. This clause was used recently by one LEA adviser for special education to justify the referral (of a child) to segregated provisions on what were patently non-educational grounds. This child needed a wide lavatory but otherwise could participate fully in the curriculum of her local primary school. So the efficiency clause can be used to perpetuate the exclusion of children from membership of mainstream schools, and by people who claim to be in favour of integration. The difference between rhetoric and reality is striking, just as is the refusal to make any explicit commitment to working towards a kind of education system which is believed to be good. We are exhorted to get down to brass tacks and not worry about the 'theory'. But how can you examine current practices and make decisions about ways of consolidating or improving them if you have no principles against which to measure them?

A teacher of children who are at present labelled 'maladjusted' fears that another of the conditional clauses in the 1981 Act may mean that very little transfer back to the mainstream need occur. This is the clause which says that the integration of a child with special needs should not be to the detriment of the education of the other pupils. Such a compatibility clause confirms the right of headteachers to refuse entry to certain children and may sanction the continuing, increasing expenditure on segregated provisions for a whole range of disruptive pupils.

The interim findings of a survey of LEA policy and practice on integration carried out by the Advisory Centre for Education and the Spastics Society show that nearly a half of those authorities that have so far responded have not yet drawn up an official policy statement, that about a quarter said they envisaged no changes in their policies as a result of the implementation of the 1981 Act in April 1983, and that only about 40 per cent of the sample anticipated a greater level of integration.

The 1981 report of the Inner London Education Authority's schools sub-committee on 'The Development of Provision for Special Educational Needs in Schools' reflects this lack of awareness both of the need critically to examine the practice of segregation and of the fact that there might be room for improvement; a kind of neutrality which, of course, actually strengthens the current system:

> In whatever setting special education takes place, it should be of as high a quality as possible both in the provision made specifically for disabilities and in the education being offered . . .. The actual level of provision in the Authority for most handicaps is adequate . . .. The Authority has been arranging full multi-professional assessments since 1975 and will therefore be well able to meet this requirement of the new legislation. (27.2.82)

As Sally Tomlinson warned, the ILEA budget proposals included spending about eight times as much money on educational psychologists (for the assessment of individual special needs) as on mainstream classroom support (i.e. on a provision that could lead to the redefinition and reduction of special needs). The staffing implications published by Avon reveal an identical strategy – four new psychologists, costing more than £50,000 a year, and '1 x Scale 1', costing £4,464 (*WHERE*, March 1982, no.176). Avon's officers see this sort of balance as being 'in the spirit of Warnock' and view the Act as 'consolidating' much existing practice. This may well be true, but it just goes to show how feeble is the official pressure to move towards integration.

And there are a variety of integration schemes which have features quite compatible with the competitive selection of pupils and the confirmed specialization of educational institutions. The schemes described in '*Integration in Action*' (Hegarty and Pocklington 1982) involve children identified in terms of category groups rather than community groups and there is scant concern for the matching of catchment areas for children with and without special needs. Very few involve a flexible resource base within an ordinary school, which could cater for a range of special needs, which are bound to change as pupils come and go, and most of the schemes preserve an institutional distinction between the unit and the host school.

So what can be done by those who are concerned for the quality of education for *all* children within the maintained sector? Richard Pring urges us to 'protest loudly'. And there are a range of positive steps that could be taken tomorrow.

What to do tomorrow?

If you accept the broad definition of integration as the process of increasing the participation of all children in the educational and social life of their local mainstream schools, and think of 'special educational needs' as those needs which mainstream schools do not, at the moment, meet, then there are a range of concrete moves which can be made towards integration and towards meeting special needs in ordinary schools, despite pressure on resources and a lack of active LEA support.

Taking a critical look at the resources, however limited, over which you do have some control may help to suggest ways of reorganizing them so that pupils who are already members of your own educational institution can participate more fully. Meeting special needs may thus turn out to involve spending more time examining curricula, groupings, timetabling, teaching styles and the present use of existing people, buildings and equipment, than on setting up multi-professional assessments to identify them. This has been the theme of several chapters in this book. Starting from your own position may reveal that there is something that can be done, on however small a scale, when the situation as a whole seems to present insuperable barriers. These efforts will be the beginnings of an end to segregation.

Drawing up a list of things to do now was the task of a recent conference held in an area by no means well prepared for integration. Within the local education authority the pre-1974 local government areas are still clearly distinct and there remain several inconsistencies in educational policy. In one of the divisions the 11+ is in operation and there is a good deal of selection throughout the LEA. The LEA officers are not under much pressure from the education committee, which has a comfortable majority, to move towards a coherent, comprehensive system. At the moment, the ordinary schools have very little, if any, ancillary help and the teachers are hard-pressed. 'Schools' and 'special services' branches of the LEA administration are quite separate. There is no adviser for special education, though if pressure came from elsewhere this might make administrative integration easier as it means one less rung on the ladder of investment in a recognizably separate special education sector.

Among the items on the resulting list of things to do immediately were:

1 Ask the LEA for a policy statement without delay. This should be widely circulated and should reflect the views of people involved at every level of the system.
2 Examine the current use of existing resources to see if more flexibility would be possible.
3 Make explicit demands for (in order of priority): ancillary help in ordinary classrooms; more teachers, to reduce the pupil – teacher ratios; more psychologists to help both with identifying special needs *and* with school organization; more clerical help.
4 Secure cover for secondary remedial teachers so that they could also work in their feeder primary schools.
5 Arrange in-service courses which focus as much on the awareness of special needs as on the development of 'expertise'.
6 Extend the 'progress classes' which already exist in some schools as a way of slowing down the process of segregation.
7 Integrate LEA administration.
8 Strengthen links between existing ordinary and special provisions.

This is a long and specific list considering that the opportunities for establishing integration schemes in this area have so far been extremely limited. Disseminating the details of schemes which are operating and extending the debates on relevant moral and practical issues may hasten the dissolution of the mysteries that still shroud the education of children with special needs and enable them to take their places in a community-based comprehensive education system. This has been the aim of our book.

References

Ainscow, M. and Tweddle, D. A. (1979) *Preventing Classroom Failure: an objectives approach,* Chichester, John Wiley and Sons.

Anderson, E. M. (1973) *The Disabled Schoolchild: a study of integration in primary schools,* London, Methuen.

Anderson, E. M. and Clarke, L. (1982) *Disability in Adolescence,* London, Methuen.

Arrowsmith, J. P. (1819) *Art of Instructing the Infant Deaf and Dumb,* London, Taylor and Hessey.

Barr, J. C. (1983) 'A pre-school community project in Scotland', in Booth, T. *Eradicating Handicap,* Unit 14 of E241, 'Special Needs in Education', Milton Keynes, Open University Press.

Board of Education (1938) *Report of the Consultative Committee on Secondary Education With Special Reference to Grammar Schools and Technical High Schools* (the Spens Report), London, HMSO.

Board of Education (1943) *Educational Reconstruction* (White Paper), London, HMSO.

Bookbinder, G. (1982) 'The 1981 Special Education Act: a discordant view', unpublished paper.

Booth, T. (1981) 'Demystifying Integration' in Swann, W. (ed) *The Practice of Special Education,* Oxford, Blackwell.

Booth, T. (1982a) *Special Biographies,* Units 1/2 of E241, 'Special Needs in Education', Milton Keynes, Open University Press.

Booth, T. (1982b) *Handicap is Social,* Unit 13 of E241, 'Special Needs in Education', Milton Keynes, Open University Press.

Booth, T. (1982c) *National Perspectives,* Unit 10 of E241 'Special Needs in Education', Milton Keynes, Open University Press.

Booth, T. (1983) *Eradicating Handicap,* Unit 14 of E241, 'Special Needs in Education', Milton Keynes, Open University Press.

Booth, T. and Flynn, R. (1982) 'Chalkway School: a remedial department in a process of change', in Booth, T. and Statham, J. (eds) *The Nature of Special Education,* London, Croom Helm.

Booth, T., Potts, P. and Swann, W. (1983) 'A community school in operation: Sutton Centre', in *An Alternative System: A Special Imagination,* Unit 16 of E241 'Special Needs in Education', Milton Keynes, Open University Press.

Booth, T. and Statham, J. (eds) (1982) *The Nature of Special Education,* London, Croom Helm.

Brennan, W. K. (1979) *Curricular Needs of Slow Learners,* Schools Council Working Paper 63, London, Evans/Methuen Educational.

'The Case Conference – Prevention or Cure?', Radio 3, Open University course E241, 'Special Needs in Education'.

Clark, M. M. (1979) 'Why Remedial? Implications of using the concept of remedial education', in Gains, C. and McNicholas, J. A. (eds) *Guidelines for the Future,* London, Longman.

Colborne Brown, M. S. and Tobin, M. J. (1982) 'Integration of the Educationally Blind:. Numbers and Placement', *New Beacon,* 1982 (May), vol.66, no.781, pp.113 – 17.

Colborne Brown, M. S. and Tobin, M. J. (1982) 'Integration of the Educationally Blind: Information from questionnaires to parents', *New Beacon,* 1982 (November), vol.66, no.787, pp.281 – 6.

Corbett, J. (1982) 'Special Care in an ESN(S) School', unpublished case study.

Coventry Education Department (1981) *Dimensions for Change,* Consultative document.

Crawford, N. B. (ed.) (1980) *Curriculum Planning for the ESN(S) Child,* Kidderminster, British Institute of Mental Handicap.

Department of Education and Science (1967) *Children and Their Primary Schools* (the Plowden Report), London, HMSO.

Department of Education and Science (1968) *Psychologists in Education Services* (the Summerfield Report), London, HMSO.

Department of Education and Science (1972) *The Education of the Visually Handicapped* (the Vernon Report), London, HMSO.

Department of Education and Science (1974) *Integrating Handicapped Children,* London, HMSO.

Department of Education and Science (1975) *Educating Mentally Handicapped Children,* Education Pamphlet no.60, London, HMSO.

Department of Education and Science (1978) *Special Educational Needs* (the Warnock Report), London, HMSO.

Department of Education and Science (1979) *Aspects of Secondary Education in England: a survey by HM Inspectors of schools,* London, HMSO.

Department of Education and Science (1981) *Statistics of Education, Schools, 1971–81,* London, HMSO.

Department of Education and Science (1983) Circular 1/83 'Assessments and statements of special educational needs', London, HMSO.

Department of Health and Social Security (1968) *Report of the Committee on Local Authority and Allied Personal Social Services* (the Seebohm Report), London, HMSO.

Department of Health and Social Security/Department of Education and Science (1976) *Fit for the Future: Report of the Committee on Child Health* (the Court Report), London, HMSO.

Department of Health and Social Security (1979) *Mental Handicap and Nursing Care* (the Jay Report), London, HMSO.

Edis, F. and Brabazon, Z. (1982) 'Inequality before the law', *New Statesmen,* 10 December 1982.

Exley, H. (ed.) (1981) *What It's Like to be Me,* Watford, Exley Publications.

Family Focus (1982) 'Assessing "special needs" – parents should be involved', *WHERE*,no.183.

Ferguson, N. and Adams, M. (1982) 'Assessing the advantages of team teaching in remedial education: the remedial teacher's role', *Remedial Education, 17*(1), pp.24 – 30.

Fitzherbert, K. (1977) *Childcare Services and the Teacher,* London, Temple Smith.

Fitzherbert, K. (1982) 'Warnock and the doctor's dilemma', *Education,* 5 February, 1982.

Flynn, R. and Swann, W. (1982) 'The curriculum at Coates School for ESN(S) children,, in Booth, T. and Statham, J. (eds) *The Nature of Special Education,* London, Croom Helm.

Fox, M. (1975) *They get this training but they don't really know how you feel,* Horsham, National Fund for Research into Crippling Diseases (Action Research for the Crippled Child).

Galloway, D. and Goodwin, C. (1979) *Educating Slow-learning and Maladjusted Children,* London, Longman.

Garnett, E. J. (1976) 'Special children in a comprehensive', *Special Education: Forward Trends,* (1), pp.8 – 11.

Griffin, D. (1978) *A Break in the Circle,* London, Woburn.

Gruenewald, L. J. and Schroeder, J. (1979) 'Integration of moderately and severely handicapped students in public schools: concepts and processes', Madison Metropolitan School District, USA; edited and published in OECD (1981) *The Education of the Handicapped Adolescent; Integration in the School,* Paris, OECD.

Grunsell, R. (1980) *Beyond Control? Schools and Suspension,* London, Chameleon Books.

Hargreaves, D. H. (1982) *The Challenge for the Comprehensive School: culture, curriculum and community,* London, Routledge and Kegan Paul.

Haskell, S. H., Barrett, E. K. and Taylor, H. (1977) *The Education of motor and Neurologically Handicapped Children,* London, Croom Helm.

Hegarty, S. (1982) 'Integration and the comprehensive school', *Educational Review, 34*(2), pp.99 – 105.

Hegarty, S. and Pocklington, K. (1981a) 'A junior school resource area for the visually impaired', in Swann, W. (ed.) *The Practice of Special Education,* Oxford, Blackwell.

Hegarty, S. and Pocklington, K. (1981b) *Educating Pupils with Special Needs in Ordinary Schools,* Windsor, NFER/Nelson.

Hegarty. S. and Pocklington, K. (1982) *Integration in Action,* Windsor, NFER/Nelson.

Hermelin, R. (1981) 'A Law to Last the Century?' *Special Education: Forward Trends, 8*(4) p.7

HM Inspectorate (1982) *The Effects of Local Authority Expenditure Policies on the Education Service in England in 1981,* London, HMSO.

Holmes, A. M. (1981) 'Segregated in the mainstream', in Montgomery, G. (ed.) *The Integration and Disintegration of the Deaf in Society,* Scottish Workshop Publications.

Ince, S., Johnstone, H. and Swann, W. (1983) *An Evaluation of a Project for the Integration of Handicapped Children into Mainstream Comprehensive Education,* unpublished report.

Inner London Education Authority (1981) *The Development of Provision for Special Educational Needs in Schools,* Report no.ILEA 1123, Education Committee.

Jamieson, M., Parlett, M. and Pocklington, K. (1977) *Towards Integration,* a Study of Blind and Partially Sighted Children in Ordinary Schools, Slough, National Foundation for Educational Research.

Jones, E. (1980) *The Carterton Project.* A monitored account of the way a comprehensive school responded to children with special educational needs, M.Ed. thesis, University of Birmingham.

Jones, E. (1981) 'A resource approach to meeting special needs in a secondary school', in Barton, L. and Tomlinson, S. (eds) *Special Education, Policy, Practices and Social Issues,* London, Harper and Row.

Jones, E. M. and Jones, N. J. (1980) *Special Education in Oxfordshire in the 1980's.* A discussion document prepared for the Chief Education Officer, Oxfordshire County Council.

Jones, N. J. (1983) 'An integrative approach to special educational needs', *FORUM, 25*(2). pp.36 – 9.

Jones, N. J., Burnham, M. and Coles, C. (1979) 'An appraisal of mixed ability teaching', *Special Education: Forward Trends, 6*(3).

Jones, N. J. and Jones, E. M. (1982) 'A school based psychological service in the Banbury Project', *Journal of the Association of Educational Psychologists*, vol.5, no.10.

Kiernan, C., Jordan, R. and Saunders, C. (1978) *Starting Off*, London, Souvenir Press.

Kirp, D. L. (1982) 'Professionalisation as a policy choice: British education in comparative perspective', *World Politics*, January 1983.

Kohn, R. (1982) 'The sixty per cent solution', *Guardian*, 21 September 1982.

Ladd, P. (1981) 'The erosion of social and self identity by the mainstream: a personal experience', in Montgomery, G. (ed.) *The Integration and Disintegration of the Deaf in Society*, Scottish Workshop Publications.

Lamont, C. (1981) 'Strategies for in-school development', *Scottish Association for Remedial Education*, no.24, Summer 1981, pp.6 – 9.

Leeming, K., Swann, W., Coupe, J. and Mittler, P. (1979) Teaching Language and Communication to the Mentally Handicapped, Schools Council Curriculum Bulletin 8, London, Evans/Methuen.

Low, Colin (1981) 'Handicaps in the Class-Room', *New Society*, vol.55, no.956, pp..460 – 1.

Loxley, D. (1978) 'Community psychology', in Gillham, B. (ed.) *Reconstructing Educational Psychology*, London, Croom Helm.

Lukes, J. R. (1981) 'Finance and policy-making in special education', in Swann, W. (ed.) *The Practice of Special Education*, Oxford, Blackwell.

Mager, R. F. (1962) *Preparing Instructional Objectives*, Palo Alto, Fearon.

McBrien, J. (1981) 'Introducing the EDY Project', *Special Education: Forward Trends, 8*(2), pp.29 – 30.

McCall, C. (1980) 'Ways of providing for the low achiever in secondary school: suggested advantages, disadvantages and alternatives', *Educational Review*, Occasional Publications, no.7, pp.59 – 67.

McCall, C. (1982) 'Some recent national reports and surveys: implications for the remedial specialist', in Hinson, M. and Hughes, M. *Planning Effective Progress*, Amersham, Hilton/NARE.

Mills, W. C. P. (1976) *The Seriously Disruptive Behaviour of Pupils in Secondary Schools of One Local Education Authority*, M.Ed. thesis, University of Birmingham.

Ministry of Education (1955) *Report of the Committee on Maladjusted Children* (the Underwood Report), London, HMSO.

Mittler, P. J. (1979) *People Not Patients,* London, Methuen.

Mittler, P. J. (1981) 'Training for the 21st century', *Special Education: Forward Trends,* 8(2), pp.8 – 11.

Mittler, P. J. (1982) 'Applying developmental psychology', *Educational Psychology,* 2(1), pp.5 – 19.

Mullins, S. (1982) 'A study of the role of the support teacher in relation to children with special educational needs in mainstream primary schools in Sheffield', M.Ed. dissertation, University of Sheffield.

National Federation of the Blind in the United Kingdom and Association of Blind and Partially Sighted Teachers and Students (1973) *Educational Provision for the Visually Handicapped,* Comments on the Vernon Report.

National Federation of the Blind in the United Kingdom and Association of Blind and Partially Sighted Teachers and Students (1977) *Response to the Consultative Document on the Implementation of Section 10 of the Education Act 1976.*

National Federation of the Blind in the United Kingdom and Association of Blind and Partially Sighted Teachers and Students (1980) *Response to 'Special Educational Needs', Consultative Document on the Report of the Committee of Enquiry into the Education of Handicapped Children and Young People (the Warnock Committee).*

National Federation of the Blind in the United Kingdom and Association of Blind and Partially Sighted Teachers and Students (1982) *Regional Planning of Educational Provision for Visually Handicapped Children.*

Newbold, D. (1977) *Ability Grouping* – The Banbury Enquiry, Windsor, National Foundation for Educational Research.

Newell, P./Advisory Centre of Education (1983) *Education Act 1981: ACE Special Education Handbook,* London, Advisory Centre for Education.

Organization for Economic Cooperation and Development (1981) *The Education of The Handicapped Adolescent: Integration in the School,* Paris, OECD.

Pocklington, K. (1982) 'Providing for handicapped children at J T Cobb', in Booth, T. and Statham, J. (eds) *The Nature of Special Education,* London, Croom Helm.

Postlethwaite, K. and Denton, C. (1978) *Streams for the Future?,* Banbury, Pubansco.

Potts, P. (1982) *The Professionals,* Unit 7 of Open University course E241, 'Special Needs in Education', Milton Keynes, Open University Press.

Potts, P. and Statham, J. (1982) 'Off Duty: educational psychologists discuss their job', in Booth, T. and Statham, J. (eds) *The Practice of Special Education,* London, Croom Helm.

Pring, R. (1983) 'Advancing the quality of education', *FORUM,* 25(2), pp.55 – 7.

Pritchard, D. G. (1963) *Education and the Handicapped,* London, Routledge and Kegan Paul.

Pugh, G. (1981) *Parents as Partners,* London, National Children's Bureau.

Quicke, J. C. (1981) 'Special educational needs and the comprehensive principle: some implications of ideological critique', *Remedial Education* no.(2) pp.61 – 6.

Quicke, J. C. (1982) *The Cautious Expert: an analysis of developments in the practice of educational psychology,* Milton Keynes, Open University Press.

Rectory Paddock School (1981) *In Search of a Curriculum: Notes on the education of mentally handicapped children,* Sidcup, Robin Wren Publications.

Report of the Royal Commission on Secondary Education (1895) (the Bryce Report), London, HMSO.

Reports of the Royal Commission on Technical Instruction (1882 – 1884) (the Samuelson Reports), London, HMSO.

Robson, C. (1981) 'A minicourse in structured teaching', *Special Education: Forward Trends,* 8(2), pp.26 – 7.

Sabatino, D. (1982) 'Resource rooms: the renaissance in special education', *Journal of Special Education,* 6(4), pp.335 – 47.

Sayer, J. (ed.) (1980) *Staffing Our Secondary Schools: a quest for criteria,* London, Secondary Heads Association.

Sayer, J. C. (1981) 'Down and up the line to integration', *Education,* 17 July 1981.

Sayer, J. (1982) *Banbury School: Special Educational Needs: Resources for Mainstreaming,* A Preliminary Survey of Teachers' Proposals, 1981 – 82.

Schools Council/Health Education Council (1982) 'Health Education for Slow Learners', *Newsletter 4,* School of Education, University of Bath.

Scottish Education Department (1973) *Secondary School Staffing,* Edinburgh, HMSO.

Scottish Education Department (1978) *The Education of Pupils with Learning Difficulties in Primary and Secondary Schools in Scotland:*

a progress report by Her Majesty's Inspectorate, Edinburgh, HMSO.

Scottish Education Department (1981) The *Education of Mildly Mentally Handicapped Pupils of Secondary School Age in Special Schools and Units in Scotland,* A report by HM Inspectors of Schools, Edinburgh, HMSO.

Secondary Schools Examination Council (1943) *Report of the Committee on Curriculum and Examinations in Secondary Schools* (the Norwood Report), London, HMSO.

Shearer, A. (1981) *Disability: Whose Handicap?,* Oxford, Blackwell.

Shearer, M. S. and Shearer, D. E. (1972) 'The Portage Project: a model for early childhood education', *Exceptional Children, 39*(3), pp.210 – 17.

Stenhouse, L. (1975) *An Introduction to Curriculum Research and Development,* London, Heinemann.

Sutherland, A. (1981) *Disabled We Stand,* Human Horizons Series, London, Souvenir Press.

Sutherland, G. and Sharp, S. (1980) '"The fust official psychologist in the wurrld": aspects of the professionalisation of psychology in early twentieth-century Britain', *History of Science,* vol.18(3), no.41, pp.181 – 208.

Sutton, A. (1978) 'The psychologist's professionalism and the right to psychology', in Gillham, B. (ed.) *Reconstructing Educational Psychology,* London, Croom Helm.

Swann, W. (1982) 'Steven: Life in a residential school for maladjusted boys', in Booth, T. and Statham, J. (eds) *The Nature of Special Education,* London, Croom Helm.

Titmuss, R. M. (1976) *Commitment to Welfare,* London, George Allen & Unwin.

Tizard, J. (1972) 'Research into services for the mentally handicapped: science and policy issues', *British Journal of Mental Subnormality,* vol.18, part 1(34), pp.1 – 12.

Tomlinson, S. (1981) 'Professionals and ESN(M) education', in Swann, W. (ed.) *The Practice of Special Education,* Oxford, Blackwell.

Tomlinson, S. (1982) *A Sociology of Special Education,* London, Routledge and Kegan Paul.

Toyne, P. (1981) 'Care in the Community', paper for OU seminar. 1981.

Turfus, S. F. (1982) 'Integration or pseudo-assimilation?', letter to *WHERE,* no.180, July/August 1982.

Tyler, R. W. (1949) *Basic Principles of Curriculum and Instruction,* Chicago, University of Chicago Press.

Wakefield, T. (1977) *Special School,* London, Routledge and Kegan Paul.

Weatherley, R. and Lipsky, M. (1981) 'Street level bureaucrats and institutional innovation: implementing special education reform', in Swann, W. (ed.) *The Practice of Special Education,* Oxford, Blackwell.

Weber, S. J. *et al.* (1975) *The Portage Guide to Home Teaching,* Portage, Wisconsin: Cooperative Educational Service Agency.

WHERE, 'One LEA's estimated cost of new Act', March 1982, no.176.

Wilson, M. D. (1981) *The Curriculum in Special Schools,* London, Schools Council.

Wilson, M. and Evans, M. (1980) *Education of Disturbed Pupils,* Schools Council Working Paper 65, London, Methuen Educational.

Appendix:
A Selected Bibliography of Integration Schemes

General (describing children with a variety of difficulties and disabilities)

Bailey, J. S. (1982) 'Special units in secondary schools', *Educational Review, 34*(2), pp.107 – 12.

Booth, T. and Statham, J. (eds) (1982) *The Nature of Special Education,* London, Croom Helm.

Brown, M. and Slater, A. (1983) 'An approach to Warnock – Sherard style', *FORUM, 25*(2), pp.45 – 7.

Galloway, D. M. and Goodwin, C. (1979) *Educating slow-learning and maladjusted children: integration or segregation?,* London, Longmans.

Hegarty, S. and Pocklington, P. (1982) *Integration in Action,* Windsor, NFER/Nelson.

Specific (describing children categorized by disability or difficulty)

Children with physical disabilities

Alston, J. (1982) 'Children with brittle bones', *Special Education: Forward Trends, 9*(2), pp.29 – 32.

Anderson, E. M. (1971) Making Ordinary Schools Special: a report on the integration of physically handicapped children in Scandinavian schools, National Council for Special Education.

Anderson, E. M. (1973) *The Disabled Schoolchild: a study of integration in primary schools,* London, Methuen.

Barry, C., Gawey, C. and Byrne, M. M. (1975) 'The education of physically handicapped children in normal schools', *Child Care, Health and Development, 1*, pp.179 – 84.

Cope, C. and Anderson, E. M. (1977) *Special Units in Ordinary Schools: an exploratory study of special provision for disabled children,* London, University of London, Institute of Education.

Crosby, A. (1981) 'Integrating Handicapped Children: one teacher's experience', *Education 3-13, 9*(167), pp.46 – 50.

Jones, G. (1981) 'Integration success story', ACE case study, *WHERE* no.166, p.27.

Halliwell, M. and Spain, B. (1977) 'Spina bifida children in ordinary schools', *Child Care, Health and Development, 3*(6), pp.389 – 405.

Halliwell, M. and Spain, B. (1977) 'Integrating pupils with spina bifida', *Special Education: Forward Trends, 4*(4), pp.15 – 18.

Markova, I., MacDonald, K. and Forbes, C. (1980) 'Integration of Haemophilic Boys in Normal Schools', *Child Care, Health and Development, 6*(2), pp.101 – 9.

O'Moore, M. (1980) 'Social acceptance of the physically handicapped in the ordinary school', *Child Care, Health and Development, 6*(6), pp.317 – 38.

Rushton, P. (1983) *The Marlborough/Ormerod Project: an integration initiative in a rural comprehensive school,* Centre for Studies of Integration in Education/Spastics Society (also in *Special Education: Forward Trends* (1983) in press).

Spencer, M. (1980) 'Wheelchairs in a primary school', *Special Education: Forward Trends, 7*(1), pp.12 – 14.

Sturges, B. (1980) 'An integrated unit at St Michael's', *Special Education: Forward Trends, 7*(1), pp.12 – 14.

Children with hearing impairments

Dale, D. (1979) 'Integration on an individual basis', *Special Education: Forward Trends, 6*(2), pp.22 – 4.

Eyre, W. and Hall, D. (1983) 'Deaf children in an ordinary school', *Forum, 25*(2), pp.43 – 5.

Children with sight impairments

Jamieson, M., Parlett, M. and Pocklington, K. (1977) *Towards Integration: A Study of Blind and Partially Sighted Children in Ordinary Schools,* Windsor, NFER/Nelson.

Milligan, M. (1978) 'Accepting Blind Children in Ordinary Schools – everyone benefits', integration after Warnock series, *WHERE,* no.142, pp.275 – 7.

Stone, C. (1981) 'Firm stand for blind child', *WHERE,* no.167, p.22.

Children with learning difficulties

Mild and moderate learning difficulties

Booth, T. (1982) 'Children with learning difficulties in Scotland', in 'Eradicating Handicap', Unit 14 of E241, 'Special Needs in Education', Milton Keynes, Open University Press.

Falconer Hall, E. and Mitchell, G. (1981) 'Provision for ESN(M) pupils in an eight form entry comprehensive school', *Remedial Education, 16*(1), pp.24 – 6.

Garnett, J. (1976) '"Special" children in a comprehensive', *Special Education: Forward Trends, 3*(1), pp.8 – 11.

Wilson, J. M. and Broadhead, G. D. (1979) 'Integrating special and remedial education in a Scottish secondary school', *Remedial Education, 14*(2), pp.91 – 6.

Severe learning difficulties

Booth, T. and Statham, J. (1982) *Establishing a Unit for Children with Down's Syndrome in an Ordinary School,* London Campaign for Mentally Handicapped People.

Fisher, G. (1977) 'Integration at the Pingle School', *Special Eduction: Forward Trends, 4*(1), pp.8 – 11.

Kiernan, C. C. (1977) *The Haringey Project,* Report to the Social Science Research Council.

Roberts, L. and Williams, I. (1980) 'Three years on at Pingle School', *Special Education: Forward Trends, 7*(2), pp.24 – 6.

Index